MY ROAD TO REMEMBRANCE

Published by Greenleaf Book Group Press
Austin, Texas
www.gbgpress.com

Distributed by Greenleaf Book Group

For ordering information or special discounts for bulk purchases,
please contact Greenleaf Book Group at PO Box 91869,
Austin, TX 78709, 512.891.6100.

Design and composition by Greenleaf Book Group
Cover design by Greenleaf Book Group

Publisher's Cataloging-in-Publication data is available.

Print ISBN: 979-8-88645-039-2

To offset the number of trees consumed in the printing of our
books, Greenleaf donates a portion of the proceeds from each
printing to the Arbor Day Foundation. Greenleaf Book Group
has replaced over 50,000 trees since 2007.

Printed in the United States of America on acid-free paper

23 24 25 26 27 28 29   10 9 8 7 6 5 4 3 2 1

First Edition

MY ROAD
TO REMEMBRANCE

A Photographic Journey *and* History *of* Over

100 Holocaust Memorials *from* Auschwitz *to* New York

FRED KATZ

GREENLEAF
BOOK GROUP PRESS

I am dedicating this book to my

late wife Doris, of blessed memory,

and to the 6,000,000 Jewish men,

women, and children who were

murdered in the Shoah (Holocaust).

Contents

United States

Sachsenhausen concentration camp

Introduction

THE DATE WAS FEBRUARY 20, 2016, and I found myself standing in the courtyard of Sachsenhausen concentration camp, in the Emsland region of Germany. The temperature was a bone-chilling 46 degrees Fahrenheit and raining. I was there to pay homage to the thirty thousand prisoners who were murdered there during the Holocaust, and to photograph the memorial. Wearing a winter coat, flannel shirt, thermal underwear, and jeans, I was literally shaking from the cold, damp weather. The thought of prisoners standing on this very spot, wearing nothing but rags, was horrifying to me. Day after day, in concentration camps throughout Europe, I envisioned prisoners lined up in extreme weather conditions for hours on end. Many of them died from the unbearable exposure alone.

For forty-five years I have been drawn to the unfathomable nature of the Holocaust and since 2010, made it my mission to photograph Holocaust memorials all around the world. As my journey progressed, I asked myself, "Why am I continuously drawn to photograph these memorials? What brings me to these places of remembrance and horror?" The answer became clear when I came to the conclusion that I feel a profound connection to the souls of those individuals who were murdered, not only by the Nazis, but also directly and indirectly by their neighbors and fellow countrymen.

My "Road to Remembrance" began when my wife Doris (of blessed memory) and I planned a trip to Germany during the fall of 1975. Doris's parents fled Germany just after Kristallnacht in 1938, and we decided to visit her father's place of birth. We visited the German Consulate in NYC to obtain as much information as we could regarding our trip. Those were the days before internet and email for trip planning. A wonderful woman working there offered to help us. My in-laws lived in Fulda, a Bavarian city, which was then on the East German border. She took a map and outlined a route through Bavaria. As she highlighted the route to Munich, she looked up at us and said, "Of course you will want to go to Dachau." I looked up at her, noticed the Star of David on her necklace, and responded "yes," and she finished our route.

A few months later we flew from Atlanta to Germany. After an emotional few days in Fulda, the city of Doris's parents' birth, we continued our drive through Bavaria. After an early morning breakfast, we left Augsburg for the short drive to Munich. It was still early morning and the fog was making driving somewhat difficult. Through the mist, I noticed a sign for the exit to Dachau. I remembered the woman at the German Consulate in NYC. We decided not to include the camp, as it might be too depressing. But for some reason, I found myself inexplicably drawn to that exit. The site was about a mile away. We drove into an empty parking lot, and in a few minutes we found ourselves alone in the camp. We didn't realize that we had entered the site before the camp was open to visitors. This enabled us to walk the length and breadth of the former Dachau concentration camp, with only our thoughts and each other. About an hour later, when we were ready to exit the camp, almost magically, the fog lifted and there was the sun. That visit became the unforgettable moment of our trip.

A year later, during the winter of 1976, Doris and I decided to join a Young Leadership trip to Israel, sponsored by the United Jewish Appeal. Along with about three hundred and fifty other young people, we boarded an El Al 747 airplane at JFK Airport. On our way to Israel we stopped in Vienna, Austria, where we boarded buses directly from the tarmac and drove to the infamous Mauthausen concentration camp. Shortly after our arrival at the camp, we were herded down the stairs into the gas chamber. As we were crammed together in that evil place, the steel door was slammed shut. For just a brief moment, we experienced a glimpse of the horror those men, women, and children endured. At the end of the visit, I remember the feeling of relief I had, holding Doris's hand, as we exited that frightful place. How many Jews were not able to walk out of killing camps, such as this one, during the Holocaust? I thought about the foresight of her parents, in making the decision to leave Germany just after Kristallnacht in 1938. They left their homes, businesses, and friends in a country where they had lived in peace with their non-Jewish neighbors for many generations. That trip literally changed our lives forever.

Germany

DACHAU

Dachau Concentration Camp Memorial

Located about ten miles northwest of Munich, this was the first concentration camp established by the Nazi government. It was opened in 1933 and became the prototype and model for the other concentration camps that followed. Dachau also served as a "school for violence" for the SS. Approximately two hundred thousand prisoners, from thirty countries, were imprisoned there, sixty-five thousand Jews among them. About forty thousand people died in captivity. Constant beatings and other forms of brutality were the norm.

Within the grounds are three significant religious memorials, Jewish, Protestant, and Catholic. In addition, visitors can see barracks, the gas chamber, and other memorials on the grounds of the camp.

DACHAU MAIN GATE

The main pathway of the camp with the museum and International Monument in the background

THE INTERNATIONAL MONUMENT

GAS CHAMBER AND CREMATORIUM

Entrance to changing room

Changing room

Entrance to the showers (gas chamber)

Inscription reads "To honor the dead and warn the living"

THE CATHOLIC MEMORIAL

Front of the Catholic Memorial

PROTESTANT MEMORIAL

JEWISH MEMORIAL

Views from inside of the Jewish Memorial

THE CARMELITE CONVENT

A small cross on the top of the church can be seen while visiting the Jewish Memorial. This has been a source of controversy since the church opened.

RUSSIAN ORTHODOX CHURCH

*The old crematorium
built in 1940 was used
until the new one was
constructed in 1943*

MUNICH

Ohel Jakob Synagogue Memorial

This very modern building was dedicated in Munich on the sixty-eighth anniversary of Kristallnacht (November 9, 2006). It is located in the Sankt-Jakobs-Platz as part of the Jewish Community Center, which also includes the Munich Jewish Museum and a community center.

It was designed by architects Rena Wandel-Hoefer and Wolfgang Lorch, who also designed the New Synagogue in Dresden, Germany. The actual memorial, called "The Hallway of Remembrance," is located in a tunnel between the Synagogue and the Community Center. On the walls, listed in alphabetical order, are some of the names of the four thousand Munich Jews who were murdered in the Holocaust.

THE HALLWAY OF REMEMBRANCE

White Rose Memorial

This small but powerful memorial is located on the cobblestone pavement in front of the Munich University building where the group's founding members were originally arrested. It consists of bronze replicas of White Rose leaflets scattered across the sidewalk. Visitors rarely come to this memorial because it is not well known. Inside the university is a memorial to Sophie Scholl and her brother Hans, the co-leaders, and a small exhibition.

The group of university students published and distributed six different leaflets, which denounced the Nazis' crimes and called for active resistance.

FUER VIELE
JUEDISCHE MITBUERGER
BEGANN
IN DEN JAHREN
1941/43
DER LEIDENSWEG
IN DIE
VERNICHTUNGSLAGER
MIT IHRER
EINWEISUNG
IN DAS
MUENCHNER SAMMELLAGER
HIER AN DER
KNORRSTRASSE 148

Deportation Camp Knorrstrasse Memorial

Just off Knorrstrasse on Troppauer Strasse was a deportation camp from which Munich Jews were transported to concentration and extermination camps. Approximately three thousand Jews were deported, with only three hundred returning after the war.

HIER STAND DIE 1883–87
ERBAUTE HAUPTSYNAGOGE
DER ISRAELITISCHEN
KULTUS-   GEMEINDE
SIE WURDE   IN DER ZEIT

GE-
DENKE
DIES
DER FEIND
HÖHNTE
DICH

זכר זאת
אויב
חרף י״י

74.
PSALM

VERS
18

DER JUDEN-   VERFOLGUNG
IM JUNI 1938   ABGERISSEN
AM 10·NOV· 1938 WURDEN
IN DEUTSCHLAND DIE SYNA-
GOGEN NIEDERGEBRANNT.

Memorial to the Destroyed Synagogues During Kristallnacht

This simple stone memorial was erected in 1987, on the site where the Great Synagogue of Munich once stood. Five months before Kristallnacht, in June of 1938, Hitler ordered its destruction. It was the first synagogue in Germany to be destroyed by the Nazis. The memorial was designed by Herbert Peters, a Munich-based sculptor. The front represents the cornerstone of the original synagogue, while the reverse side is a "protected" menorah and a Hebrew quotation from Psalm seventy-four, lamenting the destruction of the Temple.

The annual community observance of Kristallnacht is located here.

BERGEN-BELSEN

Bergen-Belsen Concentration Camp Memorial

Located in northern Germany, in what today is Lower Saxony, Bergen-Belsen was originally established as a POW camp. By 1944 the camp was converted to a concentration camp. Approximately twenty thousand Russian POWs and fifty thousand civilians, mostly Jews, died here. Most died of malnutrition and disease, commonly typhus. The bodies were buried in mass graves, which are marked by monuments. The average life span of a prisoner was nine months.

There is nothing left of the original camp. The most notable of the few memorials here is the symbolic gravestone of Anne and Margot Frank. The sisters perished here in 1945 shortly before liberation. There is an interesting Documentation Center.

(Top) Site of a mass grave
(Bottom) 1,000 bodies lie here

BUCHENWALD

Buchenwald Concentration Camp Memorial

Approximately seven miles northwest of the town of Weimar, the home of Goethe, Schiller, Liszt, and Bach, the Nazis established the largest concentration camp in Germany. The first prisoners arrived in July of 1937. Between 1937 and 1945, over two hundred and fifty thousand people were incarcerated here. It is estimated fifty-six thousand people died here, although this was not considered an extermination camp. Thousands were murdered by starvation, lack of hygiene, torture, and beatings. It is estimated that eighty thousand Soviet POWs were executed by shooting.

Original structures remaining include the main entrance, the railroad tracks, the perimeter fencing and the crematorium. There are a few scattered memorials, as well as a small but interesting museum.

The crematorium

HAMBURG

Bullenhuser Damm School Memorial

In October of 1944, a subcamp of the Neuen-gamme concentration camp was established in a vacant school building in the Rothenburgsort section of Hamburg. On the night of April 20, 1945, twenty Jewish children, ten boys and ten girls, who had been used in medical experiments at Neuen-gamme, their four caretakers, and twenty-four Russian prisoners were murdered in the basement of the school.

Behind the school is a beautiful rose garden and gazebo with plaques memorializing the children. The memorial and garden were built in 1980, and a small exhibition was opened in 2011.

Memorial to Russian Prisoners

Examples of some of the plaques for the children

Meiner lieben
Tochter
RUCHLA
ZYLBERBERG
aus Zawichost
die mit 8 Jahren
getötet wurde

Dein Vater
NISON
ZYLBERBERG

Meine beiden
Kinder
Roman u.
Eleonora
Witonski
Juden aus
Radom
sind am 20.
April 1945
an diesem Ort
ermordet
worden

LELKA
BIRNBAUM
Ein jüdisches
Mädchen
aus Polen,
12 Jahre alt,
ist hier
gequält und
getötet
worden

NEUENGAMME

Neuengamme Concentration Camp Memorial

The largest concentration camp in northern Germany was established in 1938. It was located approximately eighteen miles northwest of Hamburg, in an idyllic setting, near the town of Neuengamme. It also contained over eighty-five satellite camps, including Bullenhuser Damm. Twenty-four of the subcamps were for women. Fourteen thousand people were murdered here, in addition to twenty-eight thousand others at the subcamps. The main function of the camp was brick production and clay digging in the canals. The prisoners worked for twelve hours per day, and died due to the inhumane conditions in the camp, as well as extreme cruelty at the hands of the guards.

Only a few factory buildings remain, along with a small portion of the perimeter wall. Signs on the wall describe the activities of the camp. There are also rail tracks for the carts loaded with very heavy clay that the prisoners had to push up into the building. A museum is located in one of the buildings.

Memorial to Russian Prisoners

The brick factory & clay cart

LEIPZIG

Leipzig Holocaust Memorial

This chilling memorial is located on the site of the Great Community Synagogue in Leipzig. The synagogue was built in 1855 and was set on fire on Kristallnacht. It was demolished a day later, with the cost of demolition charged to the Jewish community. In 1933, there were eleven thousand Jews living in Leipzig, and by 1945 only fifteen remained. Each chair memorializes one hundred Jews murdered by the Nazis.

BERLIN

Memorial to the Murdered Jews of Europe

This is the most well-known memorial in Germany, dedicated to the Jewish victims of the Holocaust. Designed by architect Peter Eisenman, it consists of a 200,000 square foot site, covered with 2,711 concrete slabs, arranged in a grid pattern on a sloping field. According to the architect, the memorial has no specific meaning, but to many, it resembles a graveyard of massive coffins. Interestingly, it has been noted that the 2,711 slabs are the same number as the pages in the Babylonian Talmud. There is also an underground museum at the site.

Trains to Life—Trains to Death Memorial

This sculpture, by famed Israeli artist Frank Meisler, is located just outside the Friedrich-strasse station. There are five similar works in London, Hamburg, Gdansk, and Rotterdam. In this memorial, there are two children, representing the ten thousand Jewish children brought to safety in the United Kingdom from occupied countries in Eastern Europe. There is another group of five children representing the 1.6 million Jewish and non-Jewish children brought by train to the concentration camps and then murdered. Meisler was one of the children saved by the Kindertransport.

Gleis (Track) 17 Memorial

On October 18, 1941, a special train left the Gruenwald train station, with about one thousand Berlin Jews aboard. From then until March 1945, one hundred and eighty-six trains left Berlin, transporting Jews to the extermination camps. Over fifty thousand perished following these deportations.

One hundred and eighty-six cast steel plates are embedded in the gravel along track 17. They are inscribed with the dates, number of deportees, and the train route. In addition, the loading platform has been reconstructed.

The Rosentrasse Protest Memorial

During February and March of 1943, there were collective street protests by non-Jewish wives and relatives of Jewish men who had been arrested for deportation. They lasted until the men were released. This is the only example of a mass public demonstration against the deportation of Jews during the Holocaust.

In a park not far from the protest site, a poignant memorial, called "Block of Women," was erected in 1995. The sculpture, by Ingeborg Hunzinger, depicts protesting and mourning women. It is an extremely moving memorial.

Notice the man sitting on a bench just observing

Jewish Memorial Cemetery at Grosse Hamburger Strasse

There is an interesting memorial on the site of what was the oldest Jewish Cemetery in Berlin. It was also the site of a Jewish old age home and a Jewish school for boys. The institutions were either destroyed or repossessed by the Nazis.

In 1985, a group of sculptures by Will Lammert that were originally planned for Ravensbruck were placed next to the destroyed cemetery.

The only gravestone is a copy of the original tombstone of Moses Mendelssohn, erected on the same site where it is thought that his original tomb stood.

IVALIAKERO
KALLENGE ANO
ALSOZIALISMUS
MAREDE
TE ROMA ANI
EUROPA

MEMORIAL TO
THE SINTI AND ROMA
OF EUROPE
MURDERED UNDER
NATIONAL SOCIALISM

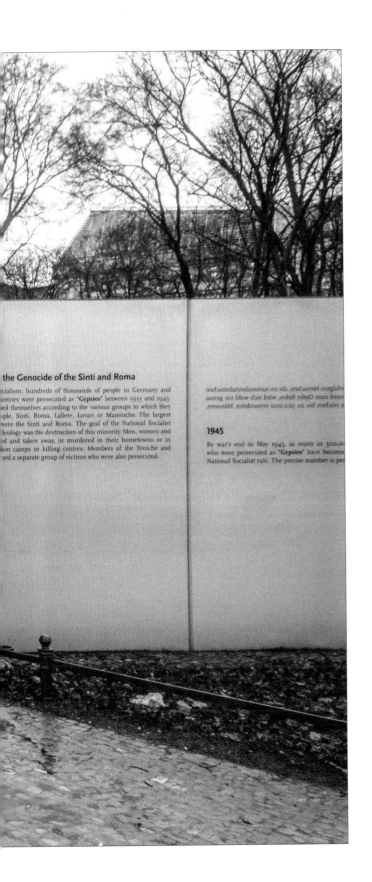

Memorial to the Sinti and Roma Victims of the Nazis

This memorial is dedicated to the memory of the four hundred thousand Sinti and Roma people murdered during the Nazi genocide. It was designed by Dani Karavan, and was officially opened on October 24, 2012. The memorial is located near the Reichstag, the national parliament of Germany.

> "The genocide of the Sinti and Roma was motivated by the same obsession with race, carried out with the same resolve and the same intent to achieve their methodical and final extermination as the genocide against the Jews. Throughout the National Socialists' sphere of influence, the Sinti and Roma were murdered systematically, family by family, from the very young to the very old."
>
> Federal President Roman Herzog, 16 March 1997

Memorial to the Sinti and Roma Victims of the Nazis

Stolpersteine (Stumbling Stone) Memorials

Begun by the German artist Gunter Demnig in 1992, the Stolpersteine project commemorates the last place of residency or employment of people before they became victims of Nazi terror. As of December 2019, seventy-five thousand Stolpersteine have been laid, making the Stolpersteine project the world's largest decentralized memorial. The majority of Stolpersteine commemorate Jewish victims of the Holocaust.

An unusual example of a Stolperstein on a building where Jews once lived

Sachsenhausen Concentration Camp Memorial

The Sachsenhausen concentration camp is located in Oranienburg, about twenty miles north of Central Berlin, in what was East Germany. It was utilized mainly for political prisoners from 1936 to 1945. Approximately two hundred thousand prisoners passed through here, with one hundred thousand dying from exhaustion, disease, executions, or horrific medical experimentation.

The camp also served as the administrative center of all German concentration camps, and as a training center for the SS. The main entrance along with reconstructed barracks, a gas chamber, and a museum can be visited. There is an exhibition that tells the life stories of seventy-four Jewish prisoners.

The obelisk seen in the background is 120 feet high and is the central monument of the camp.

A sculpture of two prisoners and a guard is seen at the base, along with a plaque, with the names of the countries the prisoners came from.

In memory of the 10,000 Russian POWs executed

The museum

Austria

Translation: In commemoration of more than sixty-five thousand
Austrian Jews who were killed by the Nazis between 1938 and 1945.

VIENNA

The Judenplatz Holocaust Memorial

In the center of the Judenplatz, lying over the ruins of the destroyed Or-Sarua synagogue, stands a stark memorial to the Austrian Jewish victims of the Holocaust. Designed by British artist Rachel Whiteread, the memorial was unveiled at the end of October 2000. The design is of multiple volumes of the same book turned backwards, representing both the "people of the book" and the knowledge lost by the genocide of the Jewish people.

Looking out from the front entrance of the Jewish museum toward the memorial. The ubiquitous policeman provides the necessary security to Jewish institutions in Austria.

Memorial Against War and Fascism

This memorial is by Alfred Hrdlicka, an Austrian sculptor. At the front of the Albertinaplatz stands the "Gate of Violence," symbolic of the granite slabs dragged by Jewish prisoners up the "stairs of death" at the Mauthausen concentration camp. There is a bronze sculpture representing the degradation of Jews forced to clean the streets after 1938.

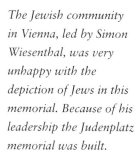

The Jewish community in Vienna, led by Simon Wiesenthal, was very unhappy with the depiction of Jews in this memorial. Because of his leadership the Judenplatz memorial was built.

On the stone tablet:

HIER STAND DAS HAUS
DER GESTAPO
ES WAR FÜR DIE BEKENNER
ÖSTERREICHS DIE HÖLLE
ES WAR FÜR VIELE VON IHNEN
DER VORHOF DES TODES
ES IST IN TRÜMMER GESUNKEN
WIE DAS TAUSENDJÄHRIGE
REICH ÖSTERREICH ABER
IST WIEDERAUFERSTANDEN
UND MIT IHM UNSERE TOTEN
DIE UNSTERBLICHEN OPFER

Translated: "Here stood the House of the Gestapo. To those who believed in Austria it was hell. To many it was the gates to death. It sank into ruins just like the 'Thousand Year Reich.' But Austria was resurrected and with her our dead, the immortal victims."

Niemalis Vergessen (Never Forget) Memorial

On the site of the Hotel Metropole, which was demolished after WWII, is a monument to the people tortured and murdered by the Gestapo in Vienna. The hotel was the headquarters of the Gestapo. The monument lies in an empty lot, and is constructed of granite blocks from an Austrian concentration camp.

MAUTHAUSEN

Mauthausen Concentration Camp Memorial

On a hill above the pretty market town of Mauthausen, about twenty miles east of Linz, was one of the most brutal concentration camps in the Nazi regime. The inmates worked as slave labor. It is estimated that one hundred and nineteen thousand prisoners were murdered here, from 1938 to 1945. Officially though, only thirty-eight thousand Jews were murdered. It was one of the few camps in the west that had a gas chamber. There are memorials from many countries, a gas chamber, the crematorium, and barracks in the camp.

Prisoners were forced to walk in columns up 186 steep steps, cut into the granite, called "Stairs of Death," while carrying large blocks of granite on their backs. They had to do this several times a day, without rest, while continually being beaten.

Israel's Memorial

There were also infamous sadistic murders known as "parachute jumps." SS men would select victims at the top and then throw them off the cliff into the lake.

(Opposite page) A large white marble memorial stone in honor of Lt. Gen. Dmitry Mikhailovich Karbyshev, a Soviet prisoner of war, who was allegedly murdered at Mauthausen in February 1945.

The Czech Republic's Memorial

*Soviet Union
Memorial*

*"O Germany, pale mother. How your sons have hurt you. So you are sitting
among the nations. A thing of scorn and fear." —Bertolt Brecht 1933*

*French
Memorial*

*Yugoslavia
Memorial*

Changing room and entrance to the gas chamber.
Approximately one hundred and twenty prisoners
could be murdered here per day.

The gas chamber

The crematorium

Hungary

BUDAPEST

Raoul Wallenberg
Holocaust Memorial Park

In this "Memorial Garden," at the rear of the Dohany Street Synagogue, sits the impressive "Memorial of the Hungarian Jewish Martyrs." Over four hundred thousand Hungarian Jews were murdered by the Nazis. The sculptor, Imre Varga, depicts a weeping willow with the names and tattoo numbers of thirty thousand of the dead.

ADDITIONAL MEMORIALS IN THE GARDEN

The Memorial Garden viewed from the synagogue

The Memorial Garden viewed from the street

Shoes on the Danube Bank Memorial

Just south of the Hungarian Parliament, on the east bank of the Danube river, stands a striking memorial to the three thousand and five hundred people who were shot and thrown into the Danube by the Fascist Iron Cross Militia-men in 1944 and 1945. Eight hundred of the victims were Jews. The memorial was envisioned by Can Togay and created by sculptor Gyula Pauer. It was dedicated in 2005.

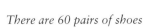

There are 60 pairs of shoes

The Carl Lutz Memorial

Approximately two blocks from the Dohany synagogue, stands a memorial to the Swiss diplomat Carl Lutz. He saved sixty thousand Hungarian Jews by providing protective documents and safe houses, including the "Glass House," a department store, which served as a refuge for three thousand Jews.

A NÉMET MEGSZÁLLÁS ÁLDOZATAINAK EMLÉKMŰVE

Memorial for the Victims of the German Occupation

A controversial memorial was built in Budapest's Liberty Park in 2014. It depicts the Archangel Gabriel, a national symbol of Hungary, being attacked by an eagle, which resembles the German Coat of Arms. The inscription reads "In memory of the victims." Critics, including the Jewish community, complained that the monument absolves Hungary of their collaboration with the Nazis.

Holocaust Memorial Center

This memorial is in the Pava Synagogue, a renovated synagogue dating back to 1924. There is a museum and exhibition center, in addition to the sanctuary. There are multiple reconstructed pews with the names and pictures of Jewish dignitaries murdered during the Holocaust.

An example of a pew

Encircling the Center's inner court is a Memorial Wall with the names of the victims of the Holocaust

Latvia

RIGA

Rumbula Forest Memorial

Approximately ten miles from the center of Riga, lies one the largest sites of mass murders of Jews in Europe. More than twenty-five thousand Jews were shot here in this forest. In 2002, a memorial designed by Sergey Rizh was unveiled. At the entrance are stone plaques with inscriptions in Latvian, English, German, and Hebrew. They provide an insight into the events of the Rumbula tragedy and the history of the memorial. In the central part of the square, which has been designed in the form of the Star of David, a menorah, a seven-branch candlestick, rises, surrounded by stones on which the names of Jews murdered here are inscribed.

Salaspils Labor Camp Memorial

Salaspils was a prison and labor camp. It is remembered for the barbarous treatment of its prisoners, especially children. More than twenty thousand individuals were imprisoned. Because of heavy labor, illness, starvation, and inhumane treatment, at least two to three thousand people died in the camp, many of whom were children.

These large sculptures are part of an ensemble of 6 statues representing different emotional reactions to the events that took place at the camp.

Poland

KIELCE

The Kielce Pogrom Memorial

The Kielce Pogrom was an outbreak of violence toward the Jewish community center's gathering of refugees in Kielce, Poland, on July 4, 1946. Polish soldiers, police officers, and civilians murdered forty-two Jews and wounded more than forty others. The apartment building still stands at Planty 9, 25-508 Kielce. A small plaque on the wall is in memoriam of this post-Holocaust massacre.

WARSAW

Umschlagplatz Monument

About two miles from the center of Warsaw, stands the monument in remembrance of the deportation of three hundred thousand Jews from the Warsaw ghetto to the death camps. On the inside wall are inscribed the four hundred most common Jewish and Polish names in alphabetical order.

ALONG THIS PATH
OF SUFFERING
AND DEATH
OVER 300 000 JEWS
WERE DRIVEN IN 1942–
FROM   1943
THE WARSAW GHETTO
TO THE GAS CHAMBERS
OF THE NAZI
EXTERMINATION
CAMPS

Monument to the Ghetto Heroes

On the site of the last location of the Judenrat is a very large monument by the sculptor Nathan Rapoport. It was dedicated in 1948 and stands thirty-six feet in height. It represents not just the wall of the Ghetto, but also the Kotel (Western Wall) in Jerusalem. The central figure on the monument is Mordechai Anielewicz, who was the leader of the Jewish Combat Organization known as the ZOB. This area was where the Warsaw Ghetto uprising began on April 19, 1943, and ended on May 16, 1943. Approximately seven thousand Jews were killed. It was the largest single revolt of Jews in WWII. A sign reads, "Jewish Nation to its fighters and martyrs."

Mila 18 Memorial

At the site of the ruins of the Ghetto Fighters headquarters, stands a stone monument designed by Hanna Szmalenberg and Mark Moderau. On May 8, 1943, after three weeks of fighting, the Nazis were able to finally destroy the last of the Jewish resistance fighters' bunkers in the Warsaw Ghetto. The bunker at Mila 18 was the largest and is the "burial ground" of over one hundred fighters, including Mordechai Anielewicz, the commander. Fifty-one names are engraved on the monument.

OSWIECIM

Auschwitz Concentration Camp Memorial

Located near the town of Oswiecim in southern Poland, Auschwitz is the principal and most notorious of the six main concentration and extermination camps established by Nazi Germany. Of the 1.3 million people sent there, 1.1 million people were murdered. This number includes nine hundred and sixty thousand Jews, of which eight hundred and sixty-five thousand were gassed upon arrival. There were also seventy-four thousand non-Jewish Poles, twenty-one thousand Roma, fifteen thousand Soviet POWs, and fifteen thousand other Europeans murdered. The magnitude of the size and scope of the camp represents the vast "killing machine" established by the Nazis.

The entrance to Birkenau

Gallows

*Execution
wall*

*Holocaust
survivor
with his
grandchildren*

LUBLIN

Majdanek Concentration Camp Memorial

Approximately one hundred miles southeast of Warsaw, on the outskirts of Lublin, stands the best preserved of the Nazi concentration camps. In 1944 it was the first camp to be preserved as a monument. The Allies came in so quickly that the Nazis didn't have time to destroy the evidence of the mass murders. The official death toll is seventy-eight thousand, with fifty-eight thousand being Jewish. Unofficial figures are as high as two hundred and thirty-five thousand victims.

The Monument of Struggle & Martyrdom

The Mound of Ashes
*Wictor Tolkin dedicated the monument with a plaque
that reads "Let our fate be a warning to you."*

The crematorium

KRAKOW

Plaszow Concentration Camp Memorial

Originally intended as a forced labor camp, the Plaszow concentration camp was constructed on the grounds of two former Jewish cemeteries. Thousands of Jews were killed here, mostly by shooting. The German industrialist Oskar Schindler built an enamelware factory in Krakow, adjacent to Plaszow. He tried to protect his nine hundred Jewish workers from abuse and from deportation to killing centers.

Schindler's factory

Memorial of Torn-Out Hearts

TREBLINKA

Treblinka Extermination Camp Memorial

Fifty miles northeast of Warsaw, lies the remnants of a pure killing factory. No semblance of subterfuge here, just gas chambers and crematoria. Approximately nine hundred thousand Jews arrived here by train, mostly from Poland, and were immediately gassed to death. In addition, two thousand Roma were also murdered here. The camp operated between July 23, 1942, and October 19, 1943, as part of Operation Reinhard, the deadliest phase of the "final solution." The Nazis destroyed the camp and the surrounding Polish villages before the Soviets arrived.

Stones symbolically representing the train station

Symbolic tombstones for the countless dead murdered here.

Holland

AMSTERDAM

The Jewish Gratitude Memorial

This is a somewhat controversial monument, in that the general consensus today is that the majority of Dutch citizens did little to resist and collaboration was widespread. The white limestone memorial was given by the Jewish community to the people of Amsterdam in 1950.

The text on the memorial
can be translated as:

Based in God's will
United with you in defense 1940 to 1945
To the protectors of the Jews of the Netherlands
During the occupation protected by your love

The National Holocaust Memorial

Originally a beautiful theater in the Jewish neighborhood of Amsterdam, it became the center for the deportation of Jews by the Nazis. Approximately eighty thousand Jews were deported through this site. Most of the original theater building was destroyed during the war. There is an exhibition in an adjacent building. A new addition to this memorial is expected to be built in the near future.

The Shadow Canal Memorials

This is a memorial that was created in 2013 by the residents on the Nieuwe Keizersgracht canal. Over two hundred Jews lived on this canal before the war, and almost all of them were murdered by the Nazis in the concentration camps. A plaque reads: "During the Second World War over two hundred Jewish residents were murdered just because they were Jewish." Their names are displayed opposite their homes.

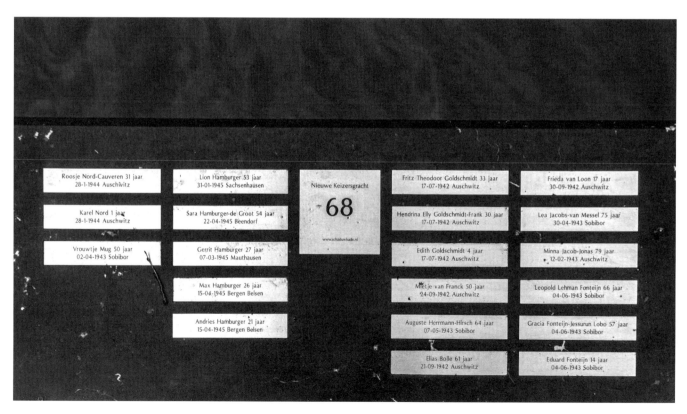

Roosje Nord-Cauveren 31 jaar 28-1-1944 Auschwitz	Lion Hamburger 53 jaar 31-01-1945 Sachsenhausen	Nieuwe Keizersgracht **68** www.schaduwkade.nl	Fritz Theodoor Goldschmidt 33 jaar 17-07-1942 Auschwitz	Frieda van Loon 17 jaar 30-09-1942 Auschwitz
Karel Nord 1 jaar 28-1-1944 Auschwitz	Sara Hamburger-de Groot 54 jaar 22-04-1945 Beendorf		Hendrina Elly Goldschmidt-Frank 30 jaar 17-07-1942 Auschwitz	Lea Jacobs-van Messel 75 jaar 30-04-1943 Sobibor
Vrouwtje Mug 50 jaar 02-04-1943 Sobibor	Gerrit Hamburger 27 jaar 07-03-1945 Mauthausen		Edith Goldschmidt 4 jaar 17-07-1942 Auschwitz	Minna Jacob-Jonas 79 jaar 12-02-1943 Auschwitz
	Max Hamburger 26 jaar 15-04-1945 Bergen Belsen		Mietje van Franck 50 jaar 24-09-1942 Auschwitz	Leopold Lehman Fonteijn 66 jaar 04-06-1943 Sobibor
	Andries Hamburger 21 jaar 15-04-1945 Bergen Belsen		Auguste Herrmann-Hirsch 64 jaar 07-05-1943 Sobibor	Gracia Fonteijn-Jessurun Lobo 57 jaar 04-06-1943 Sobibor
			Elias Bolle 61 jaar 21-09-1942 Auschwitz	Eduard Fonteijn 14 jaar 04-06-1943 Sobibor

The Dockworker Statue

On the site where many Dutch Jews were herded together while awaiting deportation to the concentration camps, stands an immense statue by Mari Andriessen. It was erected in 1952 in commemoration of the February 1941 strike by workers protesting against Jewish deportations. Three hundred thousand people joined the strike. It was violently suppressed in three days by the Nazis. It was the only protest by non-Jews in occupied Europe against the Jewish deportations.

Women of Ravensbruck Memorial

Just opposite the Rijksmuseum, and across from the Van Gogh Museum, stands a small but impressive memorial to the fifty thousand women who perished at the Ravensbruck concentration camp in Germany. At night, the stainless steel column emits sound and light signals that swell and fade away. The light symbolizes the murdered women, while the sound memorializes the prisoners who were tortured and then murdered.

voor haar
die tot
het uiterste
neen
bleven
zeggen
tegen het
fascisme

vrouwen
van
Ravensbrück
1940-1945

The Jewish Resistance Monument

On a beautiful corner, where City Hall and the Opera House are located, stands a simple monument erected to memorialize the Jewish resistance fighters who died in WWII. It was designed and built by a mason specializing in Jewish tombstones by the name of Joseph Glatt. The inscription reads:

"In memory of the Resistance of the Jewish citizens fallen 1940–1945."

WESTERBORK

Westerbork Concentration Camp Memorial

Westerbork was utilized as a staging area for the deportation of Jews from Holland. Every Tuesday, from July 1942 to September 1944, trains transported just over one hundred thousand Jews to Auschwitz and Sobibor. Most were killed upon arrival, with only five thousand survivors.

Today nothing is left of the original camp, except for the commandant's house and the railroad tracks. There are two significant memorials located here, the "Broken Railroad Track" and the National Westerbork Memorial, consisting of one hundred and two thousand stones representing the murdered Jews.

Two examples of plaques on the "coffins." Each "coffin" represents a camp to which Jews were deported and murdered.

AMERSFOORT

Amersfoort Concentration Camp Memorial

Located about forty miles southeast of Amsterdam, Amersfoort is one of three concentration camps in Holland; the other two being Westerbork and Vught. Earlier in the war, this was a stop for transportation to camps in the East. Harsh conditions and murder were responsible for many deaths here.

*The roll call bell,
which rang multiple
times per day, as
prisoners were forced
to line up for hours*

*The "Stone Man,"
in memory of all
the victims at Kamp
Amersfoort by sculptor
Frits Sieger, who was
imprisoned there*

Rusthof Field of Honor

Next to the municipal cemetery, "Rusthof" in Amersfoort, the Soviet Field of Honor was established in 1947. An inscription at the entrance reads, "On this Field of Honor, the graves of eight hundred and sixty five Russian soldiers have been put to rest." Of those, one hundred died during the German occupation in Camp Amersfoort.

Russia

MOSCOW

The Temple of Memory

On a small hill, to the west of Moscow, is located a beautiful synagogue that memorializes the Holocaust. There is a museum, a Russian Orthodox church, and a Mosque nearby.

The Synagogue structure was designed by Moshe Zarhi, an Israeli architect, with the interior designed by Frank Meisler. The museum houses a collection of Jewish objects from everyday life.

Artifacts designed by Frank Meisler

ST. PETERSBURG

The Grieving Man

This abstract monument, not far from Catherine's Palace, is located in a small, attractive square at the intersection of Moscow and Palace streets in Pushkin. The sculpture, by V.A. Sidur, represents a bronzed figure of a grieving man. It was dedicated in memory of the murder of eight hundred Jews by the Nazis near this site.

There are two inscriptions:

In Hebrew—"Their blood was spilled like water . . . and there was nobody to bury them."

In Russian—"To the Jews of the town of Pushkin fallen as victims to the fascist genocide, 1941."

Czech Republic

PRAGUE

Pinkas Memorial Synagogue

This beautiful synagogue dates back to 1535, when it was built by the Horowitz family. From 1992 to 1996, eighty thousand names of Czech and Moravian Jews who were murdered by the Nazis were inscribed on its walls. The memorial was designed by Vaclav Bostik and Jiri John. It has become one of the most visited sites in Prague.

PILSEN

The Stara Synagogue Memorial

About sixty miles southwest of Prague, next to the ruins of the Stara Synagogue, stands a modest memorial to the than more two thousand Jews who were deported from Pilsen to the Theresienstadt concentration camp in 1942. It commemorates some of the oldest and best traditions of Judaism, including respect for the ruins of holy sites and synagogues. The memorial was conceptualized by Radovan Kodera and designed by Petr Novak.

TEREZIN

Theresienstadt Concentration Camp Memorial

Located about fifty miles north of Prague, in the town of Terezin, the Nazis established a "show" camp and ghetto for the world to see. It was designed to mislead Jewish communities about the Final Solution. About thirty-three thousand people died here, mostly from malnutrition and disease. It was also a transit point for the extermination camps in the east. Approximately fifteen thousand children also passed through here, with as few as one hundred and fifty surviving.

Memorial candles for the dead

France

PARIS

Memorial to the Martyrs of the Deportation

This memorial is dedicated to the memory of the two hundred thousand people who were deported from Vichy France to the Nazi concentration camps during World War II. It is located on the site of a former morgue, underground, behind Notre Dame on Île de la Cité. It was designed by the architect Georges-Henri Pingusson.

Memorial of the Shoah

(Opposite page) 200,000 small crystals representing each of the deportees murdered in the camps

Originally built in 1956 and called the Memorial of the Unknown Jewish Martyr, the memorial houses an eternal flame that commemorates Jews who died in the Holocaust. It was restored and enlarged in 2005, and is now known as the Shoah Memorial. On a wall, the names of the seventy-six thousand French-Jewish deportees are inscribed. There is also a wall of the righteous, with the names of three thousand six hundred people who rescued Jews.

The Eternal Flame

The Wall of the Righteous

DRANCY

The Shoah Memorial Monument in Drancy

Drancy is located just a fifteen-minute train ride from the Gare du Nord in Paris. Between March 1942 and August 1944, sixty-three thousand Jews were deported to the extermination camps from this site. The monument was built in 1976, with a sculpture by Shlomo Selinger entitled "The Gates of Hell" serving as its focal point. Behind the sculpture stands a box car used to transport Jews to their deaths. Next door is the Shoah Memorial Center with a library, exhibition, and teaching areas. There is even a scale model of the original camp.

View from the Shoah Memorial Center

Sweden

STOCKHOLM

The Road to Death

In Nybroplan, a public square facing the inner harbor, stand two memorials to the Swedish diplomat Raoul Wallenberg. He is credited with saving one hundred thousand Jews from deportation from Hungary to Auschwitz, by providing false Swedish passports. The first monument, by Danish artist Kirsten Ortwed, was dedicated in 2001 and was thought to be inappropriate by many critics since there appear to be grotesque bodies lying on the ground. In 2006, the Jewish community had a second monument built, which is a large stone sphere inscribed with Raoul Wallenberg Torg (square) on one side and Aaron Isaacs Grand on the other. The globe contains the line, "The road was straight, when Jews were deported to death. The road was winding, dangerous and full of obstacles, when Jews were trying to escape from the murderers." This sentence appears first in Swedish, followed by English, and then in twenty-two languages, beginning with Polish.

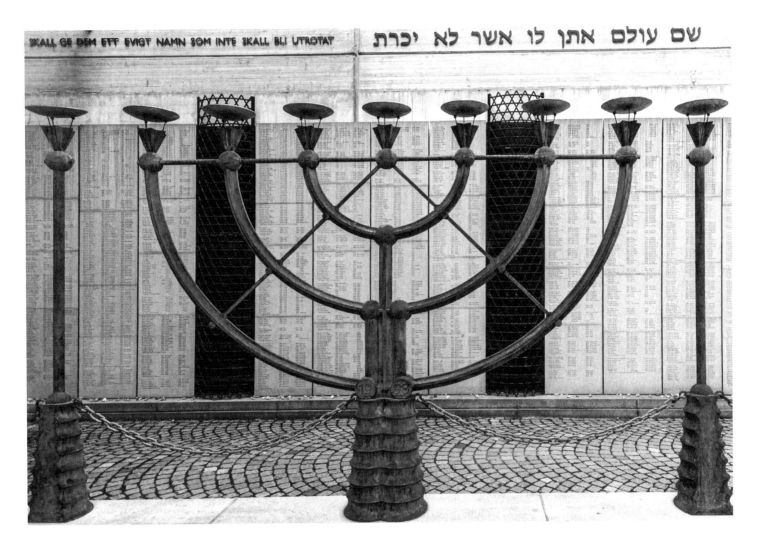

SKALL GE DEM ETT EVIGT NAMN SOM INTE SKALL BLI UTROTAT

שם עולם אתן לו אשר לא יכרת

The Stockholm Holocaust Memorial

Within the courtyard of the Great Synagogue is the "Monument to the Memory of the Holocaust Victims." Listed on the wall are the names of relatives of survivors, who settled in Sweden, to serve as a "symbolic tombstone for those who have no marked graves." The monument also lists the places where the victims lived, and where they were murdered. The synagogue is a few minutes' walk from the Raoul Wallenberg Memorial and the inner harbor area.

Joskowicz Hars-Majek	1918	Dąbrowa/Kielce	1943	Treblinka
Joskowicz Chawa	1906	Dąbrowa/Kielce	1943	Kielce
Joskowicz Keila	1919	Dąbrowa/Kielce	1943	Treblinka
Joskowicz Temera	1904	Dąbrowa/Kielce	1943	Treblinka
Joskowicz Israel	1925	Dąbrowa/Kielce	1943	
Joskowicz Riwa	1932	Dąbrowa/Kielce	1943	Treblinka
Joskowicz Chawa	1895	Daleszyce	1943	Treblinka
Joskowicz Elke	1912	Dąbrowa/Kielce	1943	Treblinka
Joskowicz Symcha	1938	Dąbrowa/Kielce	1943	Treblinka
Joskowicz Sara	1915	Dąbrowa/Kielce	1943	Treblinka
Machtinger Leib	1913	Dąbrowa/Kielce	1943	Treblinka

Zyto Regina f. Sztokman och Zyto Marek

"GLÖM OSS INTE"

ROPEN FRÅN DE 6 MILJONER JUDAR SOM
UNDER ÅREN 1939–1945 DÖDADES
AV NAZISTERNA OCH DERAS MEDLÖPARE
EKAR FRÅN DESSA STENAR.

HÄR NAMNGES 8.000 OFFER
VARS MINNE VÅRDAS AV ÖVERLEVANDE
SLÄKTINGAR SOM
RÄDDADES TILL SVERIGE

ENDAST MED KUNSKAP OM DET FÖRFLUTNA
KAN VI BEKÄMPA RASISM,
ANTISEMITISM OCH INTOLERANS

MONUMENTET RESTES GEMENSAMT AV
JUDISKA FÖRSAMLINGEN I STOCKHOLM
OCH FÖRENINGEN FÖRINTELSENS
ÖVERLEVANDE MED
BIDRAG FRÅN SVERIGES REGERING,
STOCKHOLMS STAD,
BEGRAVNINGSSÄLLSKAPET CHEVRA KADISHA
SAMT MÅNGA ENSKILDA

KONUNG CARL XVI GUSTAF INVIGDE
MONUMENTET DEN 27 SEPTEMBER 1998

Greece

CORFU

Never Again for Any Nation Memorial
(For the Jews)

Corfu is the northernmost of the Ionian islands in Greece. It has been home to Jews since the 12th century. Near the end of WWII, the Jewish population was deported to Auschwitz. Two hundred Jews were able to find refuge with Christian families on the island.

In 2001, a bronze holocaust memorial was established at the edge of town, in New Fortress Square, by Georgios Karahalios.

NEVER AGAIN FOR ANY NATION
DEDICATED TO THE MEMORY OF THE
2000 JEWS OF CORFU WHO PERISHED
IN THE NAZI CONCETRATION CAMPS OF
AUSHWITZ AND BIRKENAU IN JUNE 1944
BY THE MUNICIPALITY
AND THE JEWISH COMMUNITY OF CORFU
NOVEMBER 2001

Italy

VENICE

The Monument to the Victims of the Holocaust

In the Ghetto Nuovo Square, there is a monument by Arbit Blatas to the victims of the Nazi deportation. Two hundred and forty-three Jews were taken to Auschwitz, and only eight returned.

Norway

OSLO

Deportation Monument

Just outside the walls of the Akershus Fortress, facing the fjord, stands a simple but powerful memorial. In November of 1942, five hundred twenty nine Jews were deported by ship and eventually murdered in Auschwitz.

Antony Gormley designed the monument, which is composed of eight chairs in pairs and singularly, representing families, individuals, and couples. There are no seats for comfort, and the stark chairs face the route toward extermination.

England

LONDON

The Hope Square Memorial

Just in front of the Liverpool Street Station, in London, stands a poignant memorial to the children of the Kindertransport.

The memorial was dedicated in 2006 and is the work of Frank Meisler, who as a child, travelled on the Kindertransort from Danzig to London.

It is one of four "Kindertransport memorials" by Meisler, the others being in Berlin (Page 61), Gdansk and Rotterdam.

Australia

MELBOURNE

Holocaust Memorial

Forming the façade of the Melbourne Holocaust Museum is a memorial to the six million Jews murdered in the Holocaust. It is composed of six columns, some of which contain arms with hands reaching up for help. Sadly, none was forthcoming. There is also an eternal flame representing the permanence of the Jewish people.

Chile

SANTIAGO

Jewish Community Center Memorial

Survivor D. Feuerstein's number

Dedicated by D. Feuerstein

Uruguay

MONTEVIDEO

Memorial to the Holocaust of the Jewish People

On the shores of the River Plate, a short taxi ride from downtown Montevideo, stands a large memorial to the victims of the Holocaust. A set of railroad tracks heading endlessly to the sea begins the memorial. At the edge of the shore is a one hundred twenty-meter pink granite wall with a break in the middle, representing the break in the history of the Jewish people. It was designed by G. Boero, F. Fabiano, and S. Perossio and dedicated in 1994.

Cuba

SANTA CLARA

Santa Clara Holocaust Memorial

Although only twenty-three Jews live in Santa Clara, they have erected a significant Holocaust monument in an old Jewish cemetery. A railroad track leads to a moderate-sized monument that has, as its centerpiece, a large cobblestone from the Warsaw Ghetto. This nineteen-pound stone was donated by the US Holocaust Museum.

לזכר
אחינו ואחיותינו
שנהרגו בשואה

NUSTIOS SOBREVIVIENTES,
ESCULPIMOS EN BRONCE
LA TENAZ PROMESA JUDAICA:
RECORDAR SIEMPRE
Y ENTONAR MELODIAS
QUE SUMEN
SEIS MILLONES.

HAVANA

Havana Holocaust Memorial

On the east side of Havana Harbor stands the United Hebrew Congregation cemetery. Within the cemetery is a small Holocaust monument.

Israel

JERUSALEM

Yad Vashem

Located on the western slopes of Mount Herzl, the memorial sits on forty-five acres, which is divided into two parts. One is dedicated to memorializing the victims of the Holocaust and its saviors. The other part is used for documentation and research. The museum within the grounds was updated in 2005. There are many memorial sites here, including the Valley of the Destroyed Communities, the Children's Memorial, the Hall of Remembrance, and many outdoor sculptures. It is second only to the Kotel (Western Wall) in the number of visitors to any tourist site in Israel.

Entrance to the Children's Memorial

Exit from the museum

Boxcar Memorial

Valley of the
Destroyed Communities

Canada

TORONTO

The Canadian Society for Yad Vashem Holocaust Memorial Site

In Earl Bales Park, approximately nine miles north of the Toronto harbor entertainment area, stands a large pillar representing the central component of a Holocaust memorial. There is a wall of remembrance, a wall of the righteous, and a wall explaining the Holocaust. A statue honoring Raoul Wallenberg is placed in what appears to be a prison cell. The memorial was designed by survivors D. Smuschkowitz and P. Silverman, and the sculptures created by Ernest Raab.

Raoul Wallenberg Memorial

NUMBER OF JEWS MURDERED IN EUROPE

COUNTRY	PRE-WAR JEWISH POPULATION	JEWS MURDERED
AUSTRIA	185,000	50,000
BELGIUM	65,700	28,900
BULGARIA	50,000	0
CZECHOSLOVAKIA	207,260	149,150
DENMARK	7,800	60
ESTONIA	4,500	2,000
FINLAND	2,000	7
FRANCE	350,000	77,320
GERMANY	566,000	141,500
GREECE	77,380	67,000
HUNGARY	825,000	569,000
ITALY	44,500	7,680
LATVIA	91,500	71,500
LITHUANIA	168,000	143,000
LUXEMBOURG	3,500	1,950
NETHERLANDS	140,000	100,000
NORWAY	1,700	762
POLAND	3,300,000	3,000,000
ROMANIA	609,000	287,000
SOVIET UNION	3,020,000	1,300,000
YUGOSLAVIA	78,000	63,300

United States

BROOKLYN, NEW YORK

Holocaust Memorial Park

In a small peaceful park, at the end of Sheepshead Bay, stands a large memorial facing the harbor. George Vellonakis designed a broken tower of granite, resembling a beacon at a harbor. It also seems to contain a dilapidated smokestack. Around the monument are engraved the home countries of those who were persecuted and murdered. There is a "garden" of stones, resembling gravestones, with inscriptions of significant historical events during the Holocaust.

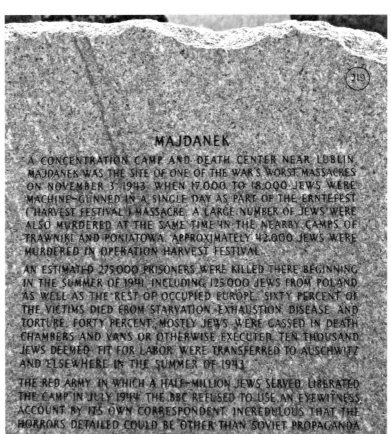

MAJDANEK

A CONCENTRATION CAMP AND DEATH CENTER NEAR LUBLIN, MAJDANEK WAS THE SITE OF ONE OF THE WAR'S WORST MASSACRES ON NOVEMBER 3, 1943, WHEN 17,000 TO 18,000 JEWS WERE MACHINE-GUNNED IN A SINGLE DAY AS PART OF THE ERNTEFEST (HARVEST FESTIVAL) MASSACRE. A LARGE NUMBER OF JEWS WERE ALSO MURDERED AT THE SAME TIME IN THE NEARBY CAMPS OF TRAWNIKI AND PONIATOWA. APPROXIMATELY 42,000 JEWS WERE MURDERED IN OPERATION HARVEST FESTIVAL.

AN ESTIMATED 275,000 PRISONERS WERE KILLED THERE BEGINNING IN THE SUMMER OF 1941, INCLUDING 125,000 JEWS FROM POLAND AS WELL AS THE REST OF OCCUPIED EUROPE. SIXTY PERCENT OF THE VICTIMS DIED FROM STARVATION, EXHAUSTION, DISEASE, AND TORTURE. FORTY PERCENT, MOSTLY JEWS, WERE GASSED IN DEATH CHAMBERS AND VANS OR OTHERWISE EXECUTED. TEN THOUSAND JEWS DEEMED FIT FOR LABOR WERE TRANSFERRED TO AUSCHWITZ AND ELSEWHERE IN THE SUMMER OF 1943.

THE RED ARMY, IN WHICH A HALF-MILLION JEWS SERVED, LIBERATED THE CAMP IN JULY 1944. THE BBC REFUSED TO USE AN EYEWITNESS ACCOUNT BY ITS OWN CORRESPONDENT, INCREDULOUS THAT THE HORRORS DETAILED COULD BE OTHER THAN SOVIET PROPAGANDA.

THIS MEMORIAL IS DEDICATED

TO THE SIX MILLION JEWS AND TO THOSE WHO DIED WITH THEM IN THE HOLOCAUST OF 1933 TO 1945.

TO THE FIVE MILLION OTHER INNOCENT HUMAN BEINGS WHO WERE ALSO MURDERED UNDER GENOCIDAL NAZI POLICY, AMONG WHOM IT WAS IT.

TO THE HEROES OF THE GHETTOS AND THE JEWISH ARMED RESISTANCE.

TO THE PARTISANS AND ALLIED SOLDIERS WHO FOUGHT FOR FREEDOM.

TO THOSE WHO SURVIVED THE HORRORS AND DEGRADATION OF THE NAZIS.

TO THE FEW RIGHTEOUS AMONG THE NATIONS WHO RISKED THEIR LIVES TO SHIELD THOSE TARGETED FOR DEATH.

AND TO ALL THOSE WHO WAGE BATTLE FOR FREEDOM AND HUMAN DIGNITY.

HUMANITY MUST LEARN, UNDERSTAND, AND REMEMBER, SO THAT IT WILL NEVER HAPPEN AGAIN.

REMEMBER!

BOSTON, MASSACHUSETTS

New England Holocaust Memorial

Located a few steps off the Freedom Trail is a unique Holocaust memorial. It was designed by Stanley Saitowitz and dedicated in 1995. There are six glass columns or towers, rising fifty-four feet, representing the six major death camps, the six million Jews murdered, and the six years of the Holocaust. In the glass are etched six million random numbers. At the entrance, on the Faneuil Hall side of the memorial, is a large black granite cube etched with the key historical events leading to the Nazis' rise to power in 1933 until their defeat in 1945.

APRIL 29, 1945: DACHAU CONCENTRATION CAMP

I WAS AN EMACIATED FOURTEEN YEAR OLD BOY when an American soldier lifted me into his strong arms. He looked into my tired eyes with compassion, shared his food with me, and gave me a small American flag of freedom.

Stephan B. Ross
Holocaust Survivor

APRIL 12, 1945: OHRDRUF
CONCENTRATION CAMP

THE THINGS I SAW beggar description . . . The visual evidence and the verbal testimony of starvation, cruelty and bestiality were so overpowering as to leave me a bit sick . . . I made the visit deliberately, in order to be in a position to give first hand evidence of these things, if ever, in the future, there develops a tendency to charge these allegations merely to propaganda.

Dwight D. Eisenhower
Supreme Commander Allied Expeditionary Forces
34th President of the United States

"THEY CAME FIRST for the Communists,
 and I didn't speak up because I wasn't a Communist.

THEN THEY CAME for the Jews,
 and I didn't speak up because I wasn't a Jew.

THEN THEY CAME for the trade unionists,
 and I didn't speak up because I wasn't a trade unionist.

THEN THEY CAME for the Catholics,
 and I didn't speak up because I was a Protestant.

THEN THEY CAME for me,
 and by that time no one was left to speak up."

Martin Niemoeller
Lutheran Pastor

This statement, attributed to Pastor Niemoeller, has become a legendary expression of the lesson of the Holocaust. Ironically, Niemoeller had delivered anti-Semitic sermons early in the Nazi regime. He later opposed Hitler and was sent to a concentration camp.

LIBERTY ISLAND, NEW JERSEY

Liberation

Standing in Liberty Park, across the Hudson River from the skyline of New York City and the Statue of Liberty, is a profoundly moving memorial to the American liberators of the concentration camps. A GI is carrying a survivor in his arms, exposing the identity number on his forearm. Juxtaposed with the Statue of Liberty in the background, the memorial sends a powerful message to the viewer. The sculpture is by Nathan Rappaport, who also did the Ghetto Heroes Monument in Warsaw, among others, including two sculptures in Yad Vashem. The memorial was dedicated in 1985.

Liberty Island, New Jersey | 271

DEDICATED TO AMERICA'S ROLE OF PRESERVING FREEDOM AND RESCUING THE OPPRESSED,
THIS MONUMENT, BY NATAN RAPOPORT, OF AN AMERICAN SOLDIER CARRYING A WORLD WAR II
CONCENTRATION CAMP SURVIVOR WAS GIFTED TO THE STATE OF NEW JERSEY
THROUGH THE GENEROSITY OF THOUSANDS OF PEOPLE OF GOOD WILL.
MAY 30, 1985

LIBERTY PARK MONUMENT COMMITTEE

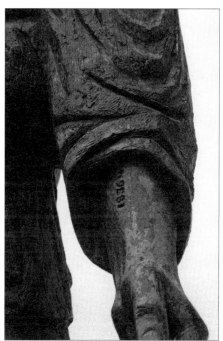

BALTIMORE, MARYLAND

Baltimore Holocaust Memorial

Only a ten-minute walk from Baltimore's famous Inner Harbor, stands a compelling memorial to the Holocaust. On property owned by the Baltimore City Community College stands a sculpture called "The Flame" by Joseph Sheppard. It was dedicated in 1988, and the plaza was redesigned in 1995, after falling into disrepair. Around the sculpture are the emaciated bodies of the concentration camp victims. There are railroad tracks, a simulated boxcar, and a wall inscribed with a quote from Primo Levi's book *Survival in Auschwitz*.

ON BOTH SIDES OF THE TRACK
ROWS OF RED AND WHITE LIGHTS APPEARED AS FAR AS THE EYE COULD SEE...

... WITH THE RHYTHM OF THE WHEELS, WITH EVERY HUMAN SOUND NOW SILENCED,
WE AWAITED WHAT WAS TO HAPPEN.

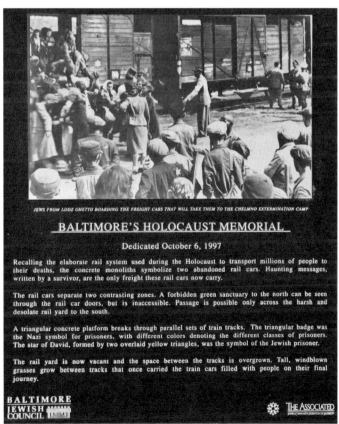

JEWS FROM LODZ GHETTO BOARDING THE FREIGHT CARS THAT WILL TAKE THEM TO THE CHELMNO EXTERMINATION CAMP

BALTIMORE'S HOLOCAUST MEMORIAL

Dedicated October 6, 1997

Recalling the elaborate rail system used during the Holocaust to transport millions of people to their deaths, the concrete monoliths symbolize two abandoned rail cars. Haunting messages, written by a survivor, are the only freight these rail cars now carry.

The rail cars separate two contrasting zones. A forbidden green sanctuary to the north can be seen through the rail car doors, but is inaccessible. Passage is possible only across the harsh and desolate rail yard to the south.

A triangular concrete platform breaks through parallel sets of train tracks. The triangular badge was the Nazi symbol for prisoners, with different colors denoting the different classes of prisoners. The star of David, formed by two overlaid yellow triangles, was the symbol of the Jewish prisoner.

The rail yard is now vacant and the space between the tracks is overgrown. Tall, windblown grasses grow between tracks that once carried the train cars filled with people on their final journey.

BALTIMORE JEWISH COUNCIL

THE ASSOCIATED

COLUMBIA, SOUTH CAROLINA

South Carolina Holocaust Memorial

Located in Columbia, South Carolina's Memorial Park is a simple but significant Holocaust memorial, which sits upon a Star of David. There are four meditative benches that surround the memorial, each inscribed with a quote from either a survivor or a liberator.

"DO NOT TAKE YOUR FAMILIES FOR GRANTED; KEEP THEM CLOSE TO YOU. NO MATTER HOW WE FEEL TODAY, WHAT WE LIVED THROUGH CAN HAPPEN AGAIN. WE MUST NEVER FORGET."

CELA MILLER, SURVIVOR

I HAVE NEVER FELT ABLE TO DESCRIBE MY EMOTIONAL REACTIONS WHEN I
FIRST CAME FACE TO FACE WITH INDISPUTABLE EVIDENCE OF NAZI BRUTALITY
AND RUTHLESS DISREGARD OF EVERY SHRED OF DECENCY...

I MADE THE VISIT DELIBERATELY, IN ORDER TO BE IN A POSITION TO GIVE
FIRST-HAND EVIDENCE OF THESE THINGS IF EVER, IN THE FUTURE, THERE DEVELOPS
A TENDENCY TO CHARGE THESE ALLEGATIONS MERELY TO 'PROPAGANDA.'

—GENERAL DWIGHT D. EISENHOWER,
SUPREME COMMANDER OF THE ALLIED
FORCES IN EUROPE, 1945

SOUTH CAROLINA LIBERATORS

NATHAN SCHAEFFER, CHARLESTON
ALLEN WISE, SALUDA
HORACE BERRY, INMAN
HENRY B. ALLEN, SR., COLUMBIA
J. STROM THURMOND, AIKEN
ETHEL STAFFORD, MAULDIN
ALVIN McMILLAN, MYRTLE BEACH
ROBERT JAY, GREENWOOD
EARL SIBBONS, GREENWOOD
RICHARD MONTGOMERY, LAURENS
JOHN BROWN, LAURENS
LEONARD VINCENT, KERSHAW
CLYDE SHORT, FORT MILL
JAMES BROWN, COLUMBIA
WILLIAM SMITH, GOOSE CREEK
FRED ASHLEY, YORK
FRED HYATT, SPARTANBURG
CLAUDE HIPP, GREENWOOD
PAUL PRITCHER, ESTARVILLE
ROBERT TURNER, CAYCE
JACK HEATON BYRD, COLUMBIA
WILLIAM ROBERT RAINEY, SHARON

GEORGE I. CHASSEY, COLUMBIA
JOHN DRUMBUND, GREENWOOD
LON REDMON, MT. PLEASANT
JOHN YOUNG, GREENWOOD
W. BROCKINGTON, GREENWOOD
LEWIS HUDSON, GREENWOOD
MARTIN WISHMAN, GREENVILLE
CECIL JONES, ELGIN
JOHN HUMPHRES, GREENWOOD
JOSEPH PRIDGEN, HONEA PATH
EUGENE KNIGHT, COLUMBIA
SCOTT HALL, CHARLESTON
J. WARDLAW, HAMMOND, SPARTANBURG
ROBERT COATS, GEORGETOWN
EDDIE ROSENZWEIG ROSS, COLUMBIA
T. MOFFATT BURRISS, COLUMBIA
EDWARD Y. ROPER, COLUMBIA
CARROLL LINGLER, COLUMBIA
CARLTON STOUGENAYER, IRMO
LEWIS HOLMES, JR., JOHNSTON
TOM 'HOSS' SPEARS, LEXINGTON
PINCKNEY RIDGELL, BATESBURG

MAY GOD REMEMBER THEM FOR GOOD
WITH ALL THE RIGHTEOUS OF THE WORLD
—JEWISH PRAYER BOOK

I BELIEVE IN THE SUN, EVEN WHEN IT DOES NOT SHINE.
I BELIEVE IN LOVE, EVEN WHEN IT IS NOT SHOWN.
I BELIEVE IN GOD, EVEN WHEN HE DOES NOT SPEAK.
—INSCRIBED ON A WALL BY A HOLOCAUST VICTIM

SOUTH CAROLINA HOLOCAUST SURVIVORS

WILLY MORITZ ADLER
FELIX K. BAUER
MARTHA M. BAUER
LUDWIG BAMBERGER
THEA BAMBERGER
PETER I. BAUMGARTEN
NAPHTALI BERGER
GERTRUDE BERNSTEIN
WALTER BERNSTEIN
HERSHEL BLASS
FRANK BRUCK
RITA PEPER CURTIN
DEITZ DEUTZ SEMPHOS
HELENE DIAMANT
MAURICE DIAMANT
ADOLFO DIAMANTSTEIN
LEO DIAMANTSTEIN
JOE ENGEL
JUDITH D. EVANS
MICHAEL FOX
MAX FREILICH
HENRY H. FREUDENBERG
MARGOT STRAUSS FREUDENBERG
RAKIEL GELMAN
CHARLES GILAK
FANNY GINGMAN
MAX GINGMAN
BLUMA TYSRGARTEN GOLDBERG
FELIX GOLDBERG

BERNARD DOV GOLDBERG
LUBA SRIMAN GOLDBERG
CARL GOLDBERG
ROSE MIBAB GOLDBERG
BERT GOSSCHALK
DORIS GOSSCHALK
DAVID GRABIN
REGINA GREENE
SAMUEL GREENE
ARTHUR GROSS
THOMAS GROSSMAN
ARTHUR Z. GUTMAN
MAX M. HELLER
TRUDE S. HELLER
RUDY HERZ
GERALD JABLON
MARIA GOLDBLUM KAHR
DENTJE KNAIT KALISKY
ANNA BAMBERGER KARESH
JACQUES KIEBEL
CLARA E. KIRSHSTEIN
YITZCHOK DOVID KOENIG
CHAJA KLEINBERGER KOENIG
PINCUS KOLENDER
RENÉE FOX KOLENDER
MAX KRAUTLER
MARC M. LICHTMAN
CHIL CHARLES MARKOWITZ
CEICA MARKOWITZ

SOPHIE WEISZ MIKLOS
CELA TYSZGARTEN MILLER
DAVID MILLER
NATALIA GOLDBLUM MOAROW
ELVIRA R. MULLINAX
LILLI PEPER
HENRY POPOWSKI
PAULA K. POPOWSKI
KATHERINE GOLDSTEIN PREVOST
FRIEDEL RAVSANBERG
BARBARA WERTHAMER ROSENBERG
ALBERT ROSENTHAL
LEWIS LASZLO ROSINGER
HUGO SCHILLER
VERA ARTYARS SENEL
FANIA SHWADHA
PHILIP SILVERSTEIN
BEN SKLARZ
LEAH HUIZEFELNER STAHLMAN
ABRAHAM STERN
BEN STERN
JADZIA SKLARZ STERN
FRANCINE F. TAYLOR
GUTA BLADE WEINTRAUB
LEON WEINTRAUB
HERSCHEL WEINTRAUB
SIEGMUND WOLFSOHN
CHAIM WOLGROCH
IRENE ENGEL ZRHS

Columbia, South Carolina | 281

ATLANTA, GEORGIA

Memorial to the Six Million

In 1965, Ben Hirsch, a local architect and a Holocaust survivor (via the "Kindertransport"), designed the first Holocaust memorial in a public space. It is located in the Greenwood Cemetery. In 2008, it became the first Holocaust memorial on the National Register of Historic Places. There are six large candles representing the six million Jews murdered. The western wall contains plaques with names of family members of Atlanta's survivors.

קול דמי אחיך צעקים אלי מן האדמה

the voice of thy brothers blood crieth unto me from the ground

דאס קול פון פאראסענעם בלוט פון דיין ברודער

שרייט ארויס פון דער ערד צו מיר

Entrance to the Memorial

Besser Holocaust Memorial Garden

On the grounds of the Marcus Jewish Community Center is an impressive memorial donated by Abe Besser, a Holocaust survivor and local philanthropist. It is divided into five open air rooms, which take the visitor on a historical journey from pre-World War II, through the Holocaust, and then to rebuilding Jewish Life.

Stainless steel table of a map of Europe
representing the destruction of the Jewish people.

After the war, survivors looked toward a
new life. Many immigrated to the
United States, Canada, and other
countries outside Europe. For others,
the answer was Israel and the promise
of the Jewish homeland. Wherever they
went, they made a new future for
themselves and their families.

Their legacy continues.

WE
SURVIVED
TO TELL
THE TALE:
the return to life

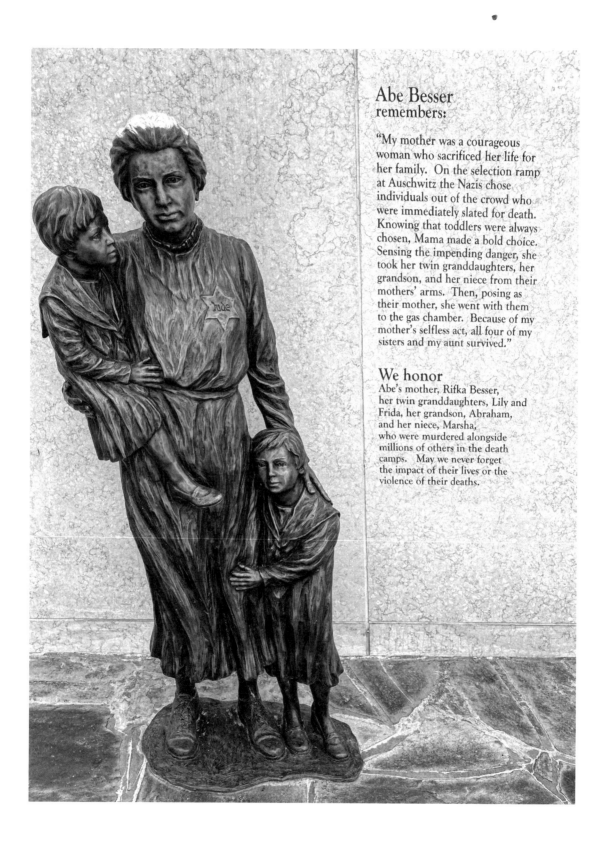

Abe Besser
remembers:

"My mother was a courageous woman who sacrificed her life for her family. On the selection ramp at Auschwitz the Nazis chose individuals out of the crowd who were immediately slated for death. Knowing that toddlers were always chosen, Mama made a bold choice. Sensing the impending danger, she took her twin granddaughters, her grandson, and her niece from their mothers' arms. Then, posing as their mother, she went with them to the gas chamber. Because of my mother's selfless act, all four of my sisters and my aunt survived."

We honor
Abe's mother, Rifka Besser, her twin granddaughters, Lily and Frida, her grandson, Abraham, and her niece, Marsha, who were murdered alongside millions of others in the death camps. May we never forget the impact of their lives or the violence of their deaths.

Eternal flame

MIAMI, FLORIDA

Miami Holocaust Memorial

A short ten-minute walk from Lincoln Road is the location of one of the most impressive Holocaust memorials in the United States. Coincidentally, its address is 1933-1945 Meridian Avenue, the exact same years that the Jews were persecuted by the Nazis. Some people have described it as "grotesque and disturbing," which it is, as was the Holocaust. Kenneth Treister's sculpture, " Love and Anguish," has a hand reaching toward the sky with over one hundred life-size human sculptures holding on to it. The memorial took more than four years to build and was dedicated in 1990.

NASHVILLE, TENNESSEE

Nashville Holocaust Memorial

Just across from the Gordon Jewish Community Center, on land donated by the JCC, stands a memorial to the survivors and refugees who settled in Nashville after the Holocaust. A sculpture of the ner tamid (eternal flame) and a torn "book of life" are surrounded by eighteen chairs and walls etched with the names of Holocaust victims. There are ten tablets containing the names of towns and cities from which local survivors came. There are also a number of powerful quotes.

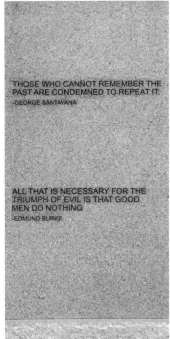

THOSE WHO CANNOT REMEMBER THE PAST ARE CONDEMNED TO REPEAT IT.
-GEORGE SANTAYANA

ALL THAT IS NECESSARY FOR THE TRIUMPH OF EVIL IS THAT GOOD MEN DO NOTHING
-EDMUND BURKE

NEW ORLEANS, LOUISIANA

New Orleans Holocaust Memorial

Located in a park on the banks of the Mississippi River is a beautiful memorial by the Israeli artist Yaacov Agam. The memorial was dedicated in 2003 and is located next to the Aquarium. It is a "kinetic" sculpture, which changes as you walk around it. It begins with a Star of David that disintegrates into chaos and eventually into hope and renewal. This memorial is significant because it is designed as a modern work of art.

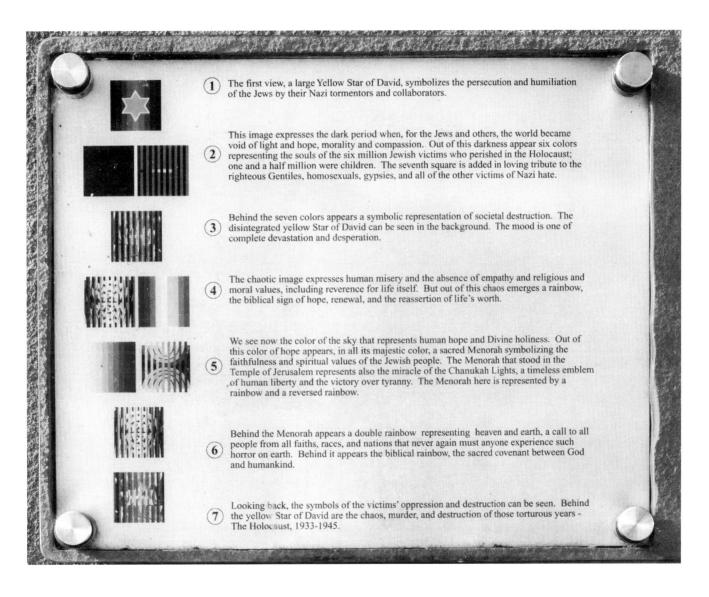

1. The first view, a large Yellow Star of David, symbolizes the persecution and humiliation of the Jews by their Nazi tormentors and collaborators.

2. This image expresses the dark period when, for the Jews and others, the world became void of light and hope, morality and compassion. Out of this darkness appear six colors representing the souls of the six million Jewish victims who perished in the Holocaust; one and a half million were children. The seventh square is added in loving tribute to the righteous Gentiles, homosexuals, gypsies, and all of the other victims of Nazi hate.

3. Behind the seven colors appears a symbolic representation of societal destruction. The disintegrated yellow Star of David can be seen in the background. The mood is one of complete devastation and desperation.

4. The chaotic image expresses human misery and the absence of empathy and religious and moral values, including reverence for life itself. But out of this chaos emerges a rainbow, the biblical sign of hope, renewal, and the reassertion of life's worth.

5. We see now the color of the sky that represents human hope and Divine holiness. Out of this color of hope appears, in all its majestic color, a sacred Menorah symbolizing the faithfulness and spiritual values of the Jewish people. The Menorah that stood in the Temple of Jerusalem represents also the miracle of the Chanukah Lights, a timeless emblem of human liberty and the victory over tyranny. The Menorah here is represented by a rainbow and a reversed rainbow.

6. Behind the Menorah appears a double rainbow representing heaven and earth, a call to all people from all faiths, races, and nations that never again must anyone experience such horror on earth. Behind it appears the biblical rainbow, the sacred covenant between God and humankind.

7. Looking back, the symbols of the victims' oppression and destruction can be seen. Behind the yellow Star of David are the chaos, murder, and destruction of those torturous years - The Holocaust, 1933-1945.

DALLAS, TEXAS

Dallas Holocaust Memorial

There are two memorials located in Dallas. One memorial is located on the grounds of the Jewish Community Center and the other within the Dallas Holocaust Museum.

THESE WE REMEMBER AS WE MOURN OUR PEOPLES TRAGIC FATE, WE ALSO RECALL THE MASSACRE OF FIVE MILLION INNOCENT NON JEWISH PEOPLE MAY THEIR MEMORY NEVER BE FORGOTTEN.

JCC Memorial

Old Dallas Holocaust Museum Memorial

HOUSTON, TEXAS

Houston Holocaust Museum Memorial

This memorial has a large "smoke stack" and a barbed wire fence built into the exterior of the museum. Adjacent is a concrete slope with the names of destroyed Jewish communities. Inside is a "wall of tears," containing six hundred panels representing the six million Jews that were murdered. In the meditation room, there is a list of the names of survivors and relatives of survivors who perished in the Holocaust. This museum was enlarged and relocated in 2019.

HOLOCAUST
MUSEUM
HOUSTON

Education Center and Memorial

A living testimonial to those who died. A place to honor those who survived, and a source of education for present and future generations.

Wall of Tears

SAN ANTONIO, TEXAS

The Jewish Federation of San Antonio

In 1990, a small memorial was opened on the second floor terrace of the Jewish Federation of San Antonio. There are two significant representations: the pile of stones containing the destroyed cities and the sculpture by Dr. Henry Miller entitled "The Last Butterfly."

DETROIT, MICHIGAN

Holocaust Memorial Center

On a busy street in suburban Detroit is one of the largest Holocaust museums in the United States. Built into the facade is an architectural rendering of the perimeter of a concentration camp, complete with spires representing guard towers. Grey metal siding represents the stripes of the prisoners' clothing. At the entrance to the building are the ominous railroad tracks leading to the front door.

SKOKIE, ILLINOIS

Holocaust Monument

Located about fourteen miles north of Millennium Park in Chicago is a sculpture by Edward Chesney, dedicated in 1987. It depicts a Jewish family during the 1943 Warsaw Ghetto uprising. In this area, which was home to seven thousand Holocaust survivors, there were demonstrations by Neo Nazis in 1978 and 1981.

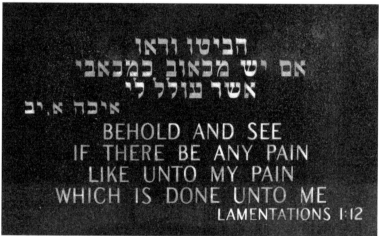

CHICAGO, ILLINOIS

Illinois Holocaust Museum Memorial

In 1976, in reaction to a planned Neo-Nazi march in Skokie, Illinois, the home of numerous Holocaust survivors, an injunction was filed to stop the march. The case was eventually heard by the US Supreme Court, which voted in favor of the Neo-Nazis' right to march. Thereafter a group of the Holocaust survivors built a small Holocaust museum on the main street in Skokie, to memorialize those murdered in the concentration camps.

In 2009, the Illinois Holocaust Museum and Education center was erected in Skokie at a different location.

Built into the facade of the front of the museum is a memorial reminiscent of the exterior of a Nazi concentration camp. The cylinder in the middle is topped by six riveted steel spires, called "Points of Light,"representing the six million Jews murdered during the Holocaust. There are two steel towers that appear to symbolize guard towers. The architect, Stanley Tigerman, was a renowned Jewish Chicago architect.

DES MOINES, IOWA

Iowa Holocaust Memorial

On the grounds of the State Capitol, stands a simple but significant Holocaust memorial. It was the first memorial on a State Capitol's property. Inscribed on the walls are statements providing historical context. There are photos from the US Holocaust Museum, including one of the children in the Warsaw Ghetto in 1943. There are also stories of the Liberators, especially those from Iowa.

KANSAS CITY, KANSAS

Memorial to the Six Million

On the campus of the Kansas City JCC, in Overland Park, stands the first sculpture in the US dedicated to those who were murdered in the Holocaust. The sculpture was commissioned by a group of survivors in Kansas City called the New Americans. It was designed by Maurice Newmanto, and dedicated by former President Harry Truman in 1963. The names of the loved ones of the New Americans who perished in the Holocaust are engraved on the back of the memorial.

TUCSON, ARIZONA

Holocaust Memorial

Amir Shamir's memorial to the Holocaust is built into the front façade of the Jewish Community Center. A large concrete tablet is at the center of this stark and moving structure. The tablet resembles the Ten Commandments, but instead of commandments, there are one hundred and fifty names of death camps, concentration camps, and ghettos carved into the concrete. The tablet has fallen into the reflecting pool, symbolizing the destruction of the Jewish people during the Shoah. The tall column represents the advanced Jewish civilization at the time, yet it is shattered at its peak.

LOS ANGELES, CALIFORNIA

Los Angeles Holocaust Monument

On April 26, 1992, an impressive monument, designed by Dr. Joseph L. Young, was dedicated in the north end of Pan Pacific Park, very close to the Farmer's Market. There are six columns, each eighteen feet high, for the six million Jews murdered. In the center of the columns is an invisible seventh column, representing the living, who must carry on the memory of the Shoah. In 2010, the Holocaust Museum and Children's Memorial were built adjacent to the memorial.

THE SAAR REGION, GRANTED TO FRANCE BY THE VERSAILLES TREATY, WAS RETURNED TO GERMANY ON JANUARY 13. GERMAN MANDATORY MILITARY SERVICE RESUMED ON MARCH 16, IN BREACH OF THE VERSAILLES TREATY. JEWS WERE BARRED FROM THE ARMED FORCES.

VIRULENT ATTACKS IN THE PRESS RAISED NEW CONCERNS FOR JEWS. THROUGHOUT GERMANY SIGNS PROCLAIMED "JEWS NOT WANTED HERE" OR "BATHING PROHIBITED TO DOGS AND JEWS". LOCAL OFFICIALS, EXCEEDING THEIR AUTHORITY, EXCLUDED GERMAN JEWISH CITIZENS FROM PUBLIC FACILITIES AND EVEN FOR A TIME, FROM PUBLIC TRANSPORTATION.

NAZI YOUTH MOBS RAMPAGED ON THE KURFURSTENDAMM, BERLIN'S MAIN COMMERCIAL DISTRICT, IN MID-JULY DESTROYING STORES AND ASSAULTING THOSE PRESUMED TO BE JEWISH.

ON SEPTEMBER 15, THE NUREMBERG LAWS WERE ENACTED, PROVIDING THE LEGAL BASIS FOR JEWISH DISENFRANCHISEMENT. UNDER REICH CITIZENSHIP LAW, GERMAN JEWS NO LONGER HAD ANY POLITICAL RIGHTS. ONLY "ARYAN" GERMANS AND THOSE OF "RELATED BLOOD" WERE ACCORDED CITIZENSHIP.

THE LAW FOR THE PROTECTION OF GERMAN BLOOD AND HONOR PROHIBITED MARRIAGES OR SEXUAL RELATIONS BETWEEN GERMANS AND JEWS; THE EMPLOYMENT OF GERMAN WOMEN UNDER THE AGE OF 45 AND THE RAISING OF THE GERMAN FLAG BY JEWS. FOR THE FIRST TIME, JEWS WERE PERSECUTED BECAUSE OF THEIR "RACE", NOT BECAUSE OF THEIR RELIGION.

1942
FINAL SLAUGHTER OF INNOCENTS

ON JANUARY 20, THE WANNSEE CONFERENCE WAS HELD TO COORDINATE THE DESTRUCTION OF EUROPEAN JEWRY; THE "FINAL SOLUTION". EINSATZGRUPPEN TECHNIQUES WHICH BY LATE 1942 HAD BEEN USED TO LIQUIDATE APPROXIMATELY 1.4 MILLION JEWS WERE INADEQUATE TO MURDER THE REMAINING JEWS OF EUROPE AND OTHERS SINGLED OUT FOR DESTRUCTION. ASSEMBLY LINE EXTERMINATION FACTORIES EQUIPPED WITH GAS CHAMBERS WERE DEVELOPED.

DEPORTATIONS TO EXTERMINATION AND CONCENTRATION CAMPS BEGAN IN MARCH; 300,000 JEWS FROM WARSAW WERE DEPORTED. ARMED RESISTANCE TOOK PLACE IN LACHWA, KREMENETS, TUCHIN, MIR, AND KLETSK GHETTOES. PARTISAN UNITS ORGANIZED IN FORESTS.

ABSENCE OF IDENTITY PAPERS, PLACES OF REFUGE,

RELUCTANCE TO ABANDON FAMILIES, OPEN HOSTILITY OR FEAR OF LOCAL POPULATION TO GET INVOLVED LIMITED ESCAPE.

AT BELZEC, SOBIBOR, TREBLINKA AND CHELMNO, JEWS WERE MURDERED SHORTLY AFTER ARRIVAL. AT AUSCHWITZ AND MAJDANEK, CHILDREN AND ELDERLY, THE HANDICAPPED AND WOMEN UNABLE TO WORK WERE ALSO KILLED UPON ARRIVAL. ABLE-BODIED TEENAGERS AND ADULTS WERE USED AS SLAVE LABOR FOR GERMAN INDUSTRY UNTIL THEY TOO WERE SENT TO GAS CHAMBERS AND REPLACED. AT DACHAU, MAUTHAUSEN AND OTHER CAMPS, JEWS WERE WORKED TO DEATH OR DIED OF STARVATION, DISEASE AND TORTURE.

ON DECEMBER 17, THE ALLIES PROCLAIMED THAT THOSE RESPONSIBLE FOR ANNIHILATION OF THE JEWISH PEOPLE WOULD BE PUNISHED.

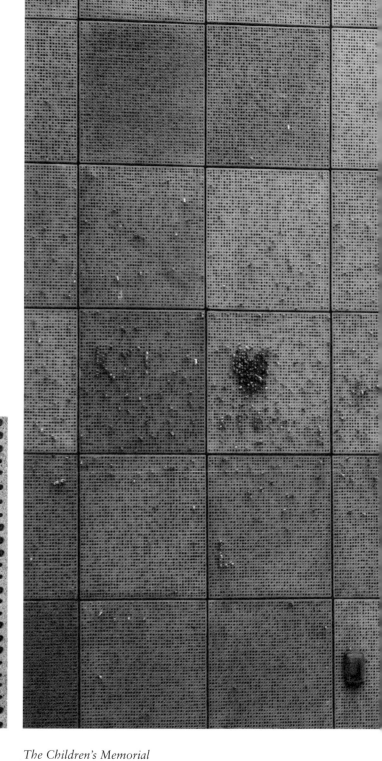

The Children's Memorial

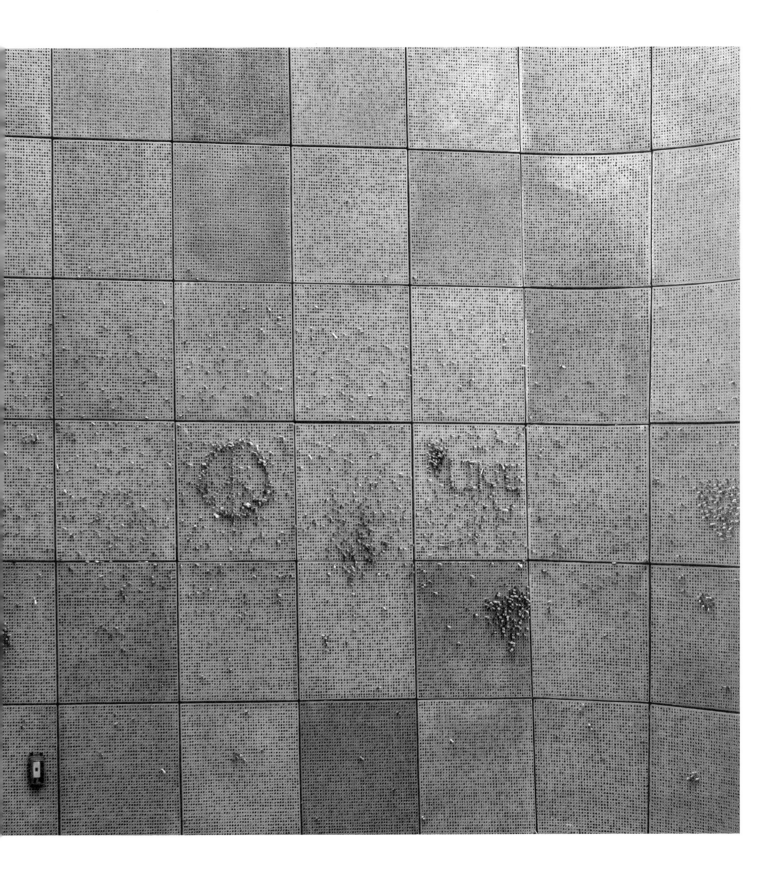

PALM DESERT, CALIFORNIA

Desert Holocaust Memorial

In the Palm Desert Civic Center Park, stands a significant memorial to the Holocaust. The entrance is through a circular row of trees, representing life. There is a history pedestal, in which an urn is buried, containing the names of twelve thousand righteous gentiles. In the center of the memorial are seven larger than life bronze sculptures, which stand on a double tiered Star of David. They represent actual victims, based upon photographs from the US Holocaust Museum. The memorial was created by the Desert Holocaust committee and was dedicated in 1995. Dee Clements was the sculptor.

SAN FRANCISCO, CALIFORNIA

Holocaust Memorial at California Palace of the Legion of Honor

In a beautiful park overlooking the Golden Gate Bridge is an emotionally charged sculpture by George Segal. It is made of bronze, but painted a stark white. A group of bodies lies on the ground, behind a man standing at a barbed wire fence. One of the bodies is in a "Christ-like" position, evoking the thought that Jesus was a Jew. There is also a figure holding an apple, signifying the "original sin" in Christianity. It was dedicated in 1984.

"THE HOLOCAUST"
by George Segal

We will never forget the genocidal slaughter of six million Jews, including one and a half million children, in the Nazi Holocaust of 1933 - 1945.

We will never forget the cruel apathy of a world which allowed that Holocaust and the deliberate murder of millions of other people to happen.

We will never forget the martyrs of that evil abyss in human history. Nor will we forget those Jews and the righteous of all faiths who resisted and fought that evil.

In the memory of those martyrs and fighters, we pledge our lives to the creation of a world in which such evil and such apathy will not be tolerated.

It is with that memory and that resolve that we dedicate this memorial.

בזכירה סוד הגאולה

IN REMEMBRANCE IS THE SECRET OF REDEMPTION

Dedicated
November 7, 1984
San Francisco

SEATTLE, WASHINGTON

Mercer Island Holocaust Memorial

In the courtyard of the Mercer Island JCC, in a suburb of Seattle, stands an impressive sculpture by Gizel Berman, a Holocaust survivor. The sculpture stands twelve feet high and consists of Hebrew letters, which in English mean "Thou shalt not forget."

THE MEMORIAL SCULPTURE REPRESENTS THE SIX HEBREW LETTERS OF THE BIBLICAL COMMAND IN DEUTERONOMY XXV – 19:

לא תשכח *thou shalt not forget*

THESE SIX LETTERS REMIND US OF THE SIX MILLION MEN, WOMEN, AND CHILDREN, ALL MURDERED BECAUSE, AND ONLY BECAUSE, THEY WERE BORN JEWS.

BY EXTENDING THE LETTER ל "LAMED" SKYWARD, THE ARTIST REMINDS US OF THE CONCENTRATION CAMP CREMATORIA CHIMNEYS.

ON THE SCULPTURE BASE ARE THE NAMES OF SOME OF THE MOST INFAMOUS CONCENTRATION CAMPS AND EXTERMINATION SITES.

PHILADELPHIA, PENNSYLVANIA

Horwitz-Wasserman Holocaust Memorial Plaza

Just a few block from the Barnes and Rodin museums, stands the first Holocaust memorial built in a public space. It is surrounded by a small park containing educational materials about the Holocaust.

COLUMBUS, OHIO

Ohio Holocaust and Liberators Memorial

On the grounds of the state capitol in Ohio stands an imposing Holocaust memorial. It is one of only two Holocaust memorials located on the grounds of a state capitol, the other being the Iowa state capitol.

In March 2012, legislation was signed by Governor Kasich authorizing the creation of a memorial to remember Ohio Holocaust survivors and World War II veterans who liberated the Nazi death camps. It was designed by Daniel Libeskind, the architect of many memorials as well as the United States Holocaust Museum.

The following is inscribed on the top of the stone wall:

In remembrance of the six million Jews who perished in the Holocaust and millions more including prisoners of war, ethnic and religious minorities, freemasons, homosexuals, the mentally ill, developmentally disabled, and political dissidents who suffered under Nazi Germany.

The following is inscribed on the front of the stone wall:

Inspired by the Ohio soldiers who were part of the American liberation and survivors who made Ohio their home. If you save one life, it is as if you saved the world.

The dome of the capitol is seen in the background

Acknowledgments

THIS PROJECT HAS BEEN A LABOR of love for many years in the making. I am deeply grateful for the generous encouragement I received from my entire family and friends while I worked on this book. As I traveled around the world on a mission to photograph the Holocaust memorials and honor those who perished during the holocaust, they stood by me in every imaginable way. During the process of converting the thousands of images to a published book, and the thousands of hours spent doing so, they were devoted to supporting me in paying tribute to the millions of innocent lives lost.

I would like to thank my dedicated and truly amazing wife, Marcy, for her constant encouragement in enabling me to finish this book. She was invaluable in helping me edit the final material and read every word.

Publishing a book is much harder than I ever imagined, and I am forever indebted to my good friend and *New York Times* bestselling author, Robyn Spizman. Robyn encouraged and guided me throughout this entire process. She has been my biggest cheerleader and introduced me to my literary agent, John Willig. John enabled me to secure Greenleaf Book Group as my publisher and has been by my side throughout this entire undertaking, caring deeply about the importance of this project.

My gratitude goes to the team at Greenleaf Book Group. They have been a pleasure to work with, especially my project manager, Lindsay Bohls, who has been an invaluable asset. At every turn of a page, my team at Greenleaf worked closely with me, helping to present my photographic journey in the most poignant way.

I also wish to honor the keepers and caring donors of these important Holocaust memorials around the world. Whether they were created in memory of loved ones, or communities that were decimated, each one has paved the way to this world-wide journey I have captured in this book. No monument stands alone, for they are all connected, with an unbreakable bond and legacy of learning.

It is in perpetuity, that I gratefully thank you, the reader. I hope you'll take this journey with me to honor the six million lives who were tragically etched in the heart-breaking history of the Holocaust. I hope you will join me in discovering your own road to remembrance. While each monument tells us a profound story of lives lost, they will never, ever, be forgotten.

APPENDIX

Dachau Concentration Camp

Location: The concentration camp memorial is located approximately 18 miles north of Central Munich. The address is Alte Romerstrasse 75, 852221, Dachau.

Directions: Public Transport: From the Central Munich train station, take the S2 train for 9 stops (about 20 minutes), in the direction of Petersausen, exiting at Dachau. At the Dachau Bahnhof, board the number 726 bus to Saubachsiedlung for 7 stops and exit at "Dachau, KZ-Gedenkstatte," the concentration camp memorial.

Visit: The site is open daily from 9 am to 5 pm, except for December 24. The admission is free. Guided tours are offered in English daily at 11 am and 1 pm, with a single tour at 12:15 pm from June 22 to September 15. The tour lasts 2 1/2 hours and costs 3.50 euros as of this time.

Website: www.kz-gedenkstaette-dachau.de/en/

Additional Information: This was the first and longest operating concentration camp in the Third Reich. It was opened in March 1933. Located on the grounds of an old munitions factory in the town of Dachau, ten miles northwest of Munich. It is estimated that between 1933 and 1945, over 188,000 prisoners were incarcerated here, including almost 11,000 Jews. (1)

Dachau became the prototype and model for future Nazi concentration camps including the camp layout, building plans and organization of the camp. The crematorium was built in 1942 just next to the main camp and included a gas chamber. There is no evidence that the gas chamber was used for the murder of human beings. Prisoners were sent to other camps to be murdered, although there were summary executions by firing squad and hangings.(2) So why was there a gas chamber? It is thought that it was used for training purposes. No extermination camps were placed in Germany. (4)

The camp mainly functioned as a forced labor camp in various industries, such as armaments and road construction. As in other Nazi concentration camps, medical experiments were performed on prisoners. Hundreds of prisoners died and were maimed at the hands of German physicians. (2)

Over three thousand religious practitioners, including deacons, bishops, and priests were also imprisoned here. It was considered a central camp for Christian religious inmates. (2)

In early 1945, as the Allies advanced toward Germany, prisoners were transferred here from other camps. They often arrived near death, from a lack of fluids and food. Typhus was common because of the lack of hygiene, the crowded conditions, and the poor general health of the prisoners. (2)

On April 29, 1945 the concentration camp was surrendered to the Rainbow Division of the Seventh American Army without a shot being fired. (3) Approximately thirty-two thousand prisoners were liberated. Thirty railroad cars filled with bodies were found near the camp. (2)

Ohel Jakob Synagogue Memorial

Location: The synagogue is located very close to the tourist area in Munich, which includes the famous Rathaus-Glockenspiel. The address is Sankt-Jakobs-Platz 18, 80331 Munchen.

Directions: It is only a 6 or 7 minute walk from the Rathaus-Glockenspiel to the synagogue. Head west on Marienplatz toward Weinstraße, continue onto

Rosenstrsse, turn right onto Rindermarket and then left onto Seldinger Str. Then turn left onto Dultsrasse and continue on Sankt-Jakobs-Platz.

Visit: The synagogue and the memorial are open to the public. The hours are from 8:30 am to 6 pm Sunday through Thursday and Friday from 8:30 am to 3 pm. The synagogue is open for prayers on Shabbat as well.

Website: www.germany.travel/en/towns-cities-culture/ jewish-traveler/big-cities/munich.html

Additional Information: Designed by architects Rena Wandel-Hoefer and Wolfgang Lorch, who also designed the New Synagogue in Dresden, Germany, Ohel Jakob is an ultramodern structure. It stands in the Sankt-Jakobs-Platz adjacent to the Jewish Community Center and the Jewish Museum. The synagogue faces east and contains 800 seats. It is in the shape of a cube made of steel and glass set on a stone base. "There are multiple layers of glass covered in a bronze mesh, which symbolizes the tents used by the Israelites in the wilderness." (5)

The entrance to the synagogue is through the "Tunnel of Remembrance," which contains the 4,300 names of Munich Jews murdered between 1933 and 1945. The names are inscribed on a backlit wall with some names more visible than others. As one ascends through the tunnel, you eventually come into the foyer of the synagogue and the light of its transparent ceiling.

The White Rose Memorial

Location: The sidewalk memorial and exhibition is located at the Ludwig-Maxmilians University at Geschwister-Scholl-Platz 1, 80539 Munchen.

Directions: From the Marienplatz station take the U3 toward Moosach for 2 stops to University station and walk about 3 minutes to the sidewalk memorial.

Website: www.weisse-rose-stiftung.de/ white-rose-memorial-exhibition

Visit: The outdoor ground memorial is always visible. The exhibition is open Monday to Friday from 10 am to 5 pm and on Saturday from 11:30 am to 4:30 pm.

Additional Information: While attending the University of Munich, a group of students, led by Hans and Sophie Scholl, printed and distributed resistance pamphlets in the Munich area. They were then copied and distributed throughout southern Germany. Six leaflets were produced denouncing the Nazi regime and the persecution and mass murder of Jews. Approximately fifteen thousand copies were made. They operated for about eight months until they were arrested by the Gestapo on February 22nd, 1943. Hans, Sophie, and Christoph Probst were executed four days after they were arrested. (8)

In addition to the plaques on the ground, there is a permanent exhibition in the Ludwig-Maximilian University. There is no fee. (9)

Deportation Camp Knorrstrasse Memorial

Location: The memorial is located in Milbertshofen, a northern suburb of Munich, just inside the Frankfurter Ring.

Directions: At the Munich Marienplatz station, take the U6 toward Klinikum Grosshadern for just one stop to Seldinger Tor. Change to the U2 in the direction of Feldmoching, for 9 stops to Am Hart. Walk for about one minute to the memorial on Troppauer Str.

Visit: This is an outdoor public monument and can be visited anytime.

Additional Information: This monument memorializes the Milbertshofen Deportation Camp, which was utilized to deport Munich's Jewish population. During the spring of 1941, the Jewish community was forced to build a camp in the northern suburbs of Milbertshofen. Up to eleven hundred Jews were held here for deportation during November 1941. Of the three thousand Jews deported, only three hundred returned after the war.

Memorial to the Destroyed Synagogues During Kristallnacht

Location: The memorial is located near the corner of Maxburgstrasse and Herzog-Max-Strasse, approximately a 10-minute walk from the Old Town in Munich, Germany.

Directions: From Old Town head west on Maffeistrasse towards Windenmacherstrasse and turn left for 71 m. Turn right onto Lowengrube for 70 m, then a slight left on Augustinerstrasse for 150 m, and turn right onto Herzog-Max-Strasse.

Visit: This is an outdoor public monument and can be visited anytime.

Additional Information: The official reason for the destruction of the synagogue was that it interfered with a city construction project. It is believed that Hitler wanted it removed because it was very close to his favorite nightclub in the Kunstlerhaus (Artists' House).

Bergen-Belsen Concentration Camp

Location: The camp is located in northern Germany in an area called Lower Saxony.

Directions: From Hamburg it is about a one hour and ten minute drive to the camp site. Drive south on the B5 to the A255 and then to the A1 to the A7, and then to the B3, to Bergen. Then follow the L298 to the site.

Visit: The camp is open every day from 10:30 am to 4 pm, from October to March, and stays open until 5 pm from April to September. In addition to the grounds, which contain burial plots and a few memorials, there is a Documentation and Visitor Center. There is also a memorial to Margot and Anne Frank. Approximately two and a half hours is recommended

for the site visit. Guided tours are offered for three euros.

Website: https://bergen-belsen.stiftung-ng.de/en/your-visit/

Additional Information: It is estimated that 120,000 prisoners passed through here. There were no gas chambers. The treatment of the prisoners was less harsh than in the other camps because the Germans thought they might be able to use the prisoners for a prisoner exchange. It is estimated that more than 50,000 deaths occurred, mostly from disease and malnutrition. (10) Only 2,560 Jewish prisoners were actually ever released. (10) In August of 1944, a women's camp was created, and by the end of the year approximately 9,000 women and young girls were imprisoned here. Margot and Anne Frank died here in February or March of 1945.

Buchenwald Concentration Camp

Location: The camp is located 60 miles south of Hamburg, Germany.

Directions: From Hamburg it is about a one hour and ten minute drive to the camp site. Drive south on B5 to A255 and then to A1 to A7 to B3 Bergen. Then follow L298 to the site at Anne-Frank-Platz, 29303 Lohheide, Germany.

Visit: The visitor center is open during April–October from Tuesday to Sunday from 9:00 am–6:20 pm. During November–March it is open from Tuesday to Sunday from 9:00 am–4:20 pm. The center is closed on Monday.

There is no entrance fee.

Telephone: +49 (0)3643 430 200

Website: www.buchenwald.de

Additional Information: Established in July 1937, this

was one of the first camps and the largest concentration camp within Germany. The first prisoners were suspected communists. Eventually Jews, Poles, Romani people, freemasons, mentally and physically disabled people, and POWs were interned here. There were also common criminals and "sexual deviants" among the prisoners. Almost all worked as forced labor in local armament factories. The camp was liberated by the U.S. Army in April 1945. One of its subcamps was visited by Dwight D. Eisenhower. (11)

Bullenhuser Damm School Memorial

Location: The memorial is located approximately 3 miles southeast of the Hamburg Central train station.

Directions: From the main train station in Hamburg it is about a 10-minute bus ride on the #3 bus toward Kraftwerk Tiefstack (4 stops) and then a 17-minute walk to 92-92 Bullenhuser Damm 20539, Hamburg.

Visit: The outdoor memorial can be visited anytime, but the indoor memorial is only open on Sunday from 10 am to 5 pm, and is free.

Website: http://www.kinder-vom-bullenhuser-damm. de/_english/the_memorial.php

Additional Information: Kurt Heissmeyer, an SS physician, injected Jewish children with live TB bacilli in order to produce a vaccine. Ten boys and ten girls were selected by Josef Mengele at the Auschwitz concentration camp and sent to Hamburg. A Polish-born Jewish doctor, Paula Trocki, accompanied the children and survived the war. She was able to give testimony in Jerusalem to what she had witnessed. (12)

Neuengamme Concentration Camp

Location: The camp is 18 miles northwest of Hamburg in the town of Neuengamme at Neuengammer Hausdeich Brücke, 21039 Hamburg.

Directions: The drive from Hamburg is only 25 minutes compared to up to 2 hours by public transportation and walking. From Hamburg take Ring road 1 to A25. Take exit 6 and continue on Curslacker Heerwig Drive for 6 minutes and arrive at Neuengammer Hausdeich Brücke.

If you are coming by bus, take bus 227 or 327 from Bergedorf station in Hamburg.

Visit: The site is open Monday to Friday from 9:30 am to 4 pm and on Saturday and Sunday from noon to 5 pm (October to March) and noon to 7 pm (April to September). Admission is free.

Telephone: +49 40 428 131 500

Website: https://www.kz-gedenkstaette-neuengamme. de/en/

Leipzig Holocaust Memorial

Location: The memorial is located centrally in Leipzig at Zentralstrasse 4, 04109 Leipzig, Germany.

Directions: It is a short 6-minute walk from the city hall. Walk south on Katherinenstrasse for one block and turn right on Thomasgasse. Walk about 4 blocks and turn left on Zentralstrasse to Zentralstrasse 4.

Visit: This is an outdoor memorial and can be visited at any time. It is illuminated at night.

Website: https://jguideeurope.org/en/site/ holocaust-memorial-of-leipzig/

Additional Information: In 1938, during Kristallnacht, 553 Jewish men were arrested and many Jewish structures were destroyed. The memorial is on the original site of the Moorish Revival Leipzig synagogue. Deportations began during January of 1942, and lasted until the last Jews were deported to Theresienstadt in February 1945.

Memorial to the Murdered Jews of Europe

Location: The memorial is located about one block from the Brandenburg Gate in Berlin, Germany.

Directions: Just walk south on Eberstrasse and you will see the memorial.

Visit: This is an outdoor memorial and can be visited anytime. There is an interesting information center that is open from April to September on Tuesday to Sunday from 10 am to 8 pm, and from October to March on Tuesday to Sunday from 10 am to 7 pm.

Website: https://www.stiftung-denkmal.de/

Additional Information: In the information center there is a display of the timeline of the Final Solution. There are also four rooms dedicated to personal aspects of the Holocaust. There is a room of names, in which the names of the victims are read out loud, and a room of families, which details the fate of fifteen Jewish families.

Trains to Life—Trains to Death

Location: The memorial is located just outside the Friedrichstrasse station on Georgenstrass in Berlin, Germany.

Directions: It is a 12-minute walk from the Brandenburg gate to the memorial. Head west on Pariser Paltz onto Unter den Linden for about 500 meters. Turn left onto Neustadtishe Kirchstrasse and after 300 meters turn right on Geogenstrasse. The memorial is just in front of the entrance to the U-Bahn.

Visit: This is an outdoor monument so it can be visited at any time.

Website: https://www.visitberlin.de/en/trains-life-trains-death-0

Additional Information: A London stockbroker, Nicholas Winton, worked with his fellow Brits to bring the first rescued children to the U.K. They left from the Friedrichstrasse station with 196 children on November 30, 1938.

Gleis (Track) 17 Memorial

Location: The memorial is located in Grunewald, a western suburb of Berlin, Germany.

Directions: Take the S-Bahn (above ground train) S7 from the Berlin Friedrichstrasse station toward Potsdam for 8 stops, to the Berlin-Grunewald station. Walk about 2 minutes to the platform 17. The trip takes about 30 minutes.

Visit: This is an outdoor memorial and can be visited anytime.

Website: https://www.memorialmuseums.org/eng/staettens/view/338/Mahnmal-Gleis-17-—-Berlin-Grunewald

The Rosenstrasse Protest Memorial

Location: A short drive east of the Brandenburg Gate in Berlin, Germany.

Directions: From the Brandenburger Tor bus station take the 245 bus toward Alexanderplatz for 4 stops. Exit at Spandauer Str./ Marienkircje and walk for about 2 minutes to the park.

Visit: This is an outdoor monument so it can be visited at any time.

Website: https://www.visitberlin.de/en/block-women

Additional Information: The memorial is built on the former site of the Old Synagogue, which was destroyed during the Holocaust. The sculpture is actually titled, "The Block of Women." During the roundups of Jews in Berlin, some two thousand Jews, mostly men, who were married to non-Jewish spouses, were imprisoned in a building on Rosen-strasse. For a week, some six hundred women were involved in daily protests until they were released. None of the protesters were ever punished.

The Jewish Memorial Cemetery at Grosse Hamburger Strasse

Location: It is approximately a 15-minute train ride to Grosse Hamburger Str. 26, 10115 Berlin, Germany.

Directions: From the Brandenburger Tor S-Bahn train station take the S2 toward S Buch for 2 stops. Exit at Oranienburger Strasse and walk about 600 meters to the cemetery.

Visit: This is an outdoor monument so it can be visited at any time.

Website: http://www.jg-berlin.org/en/judaism/cemeteries/grosse-hamburger-strasse.html

Additional Information: In 1943, the Gestapo ordered the cemetery to be destroyed. The Nazis desecrated the graves and used the tombstones to build an air raid shelter. In April 1945, three thousand victims of air raids were buried here alongside approximately three thousand Jewish dead. A Jewish school was also located adjacent to the cemetery and this was reopened as a middle and high school by the Jewish community in 1993. (13)

Memorial to the Sinti and Roma Victims of the Nazis

Location: The memorial is located just a few blocks northwest of the Brandenburg Gate near the Reichstag in Berlin, Germany.

Directions: From the Brandenburg Gate head north on Paiser Platz and then turn left toward Ebertstrasse.

Turn right on Eibertstrasse and then left on Scheide-mannstrasse and you will see the memorial.

Visit: This is an outdoor monument so it can be visited at any time.

Website: https://www.visitberlin.de/en/sinti-and-roma-memorial

Additional Information: There were approximately nine hundred and fifty thousand Romani living in countries controlled by the Nazis. The Nuremberg racial laws did not mention Romani, but they were considered, along with Jews and Black people, as "racially distinctive minorities with alien blood."(14)

Sachsenhausen Concentration Camp

Location: The camp is located approximately 20 miles north of Central Berlin, Germany.

Directions: Take the S1 from the Berlin-Gesundbrunnen station to Oranienburg, about a 20-minute ride, and then walk for about 20 minutes to the memorial and camp.

Visit: The outside areas are open daily from 8:30 am to 6 pm, with the visitor's center open from 8:30am to 5pm, with a break for lunch between 1 and 1:30. Admission is free. Guided tours are available for a small fee.

Sachsenhausen Memorial and Museum Straße der Nationen 22 D-16515 Oranienburg

Telephone: +49 (0)3301 200-0.

Website: https://www.sachsenhausen-sbg.de/en/visitor-service/

Additional Information: On April 21, 1945, thirty thousand prisoners were evacuated from the camp on a Death March toward the northwest. Thousands died on the March. The camp was liberated on April 22,

1945, by units of the Soviet and Polish Army. They found three thousand sick prisoners along with doctors and nurses. Three hundred of these prisoners did not survive, and were buried in mass graves near the infirmary. (15)

The Judenplatz Holocaust Memorial

Location: The memorial is located about a 15-minute walk just north of the Hotel Sacher, a landmark hotel in Vienna, Austria.

Directions: Walk north on Karntner Str. for 450 meters and then turn left onto Graben. Continue for 300 meters and turn right onto Seitzergasse.

Visit: This is an outdoor sculpture and is always open.

Website: https://www.visitingvienna.com/sights/museums/holocaust-memorial/

The Memorial Against War and Fascism

Location: The memorial is located just opposite the Sacher Hotel in central Vienna, Austria.

Directions: Opposite the Hotel Sacher in the Albertinaplatz.

Visit: This is an outdoor sculpture and is always open.

Website: https://war-documentary.info/vienna-monument-against-fascism/

Additional Information: There are four main parts to this memorial. It has been described as a "walking-in" memorial as you literally walk through it. The first part is a simple stone engraved with the following words, "This monument is dedicated to all victims of war and fascism."

There is no particular mention of the Jewish people or other specific groups murdered by the Nazis. You then pass through the "Gates of Violence" and come

upon a bronze statue, which depicts an older man, a Jew, in a humiliating position. You then encounter a man transfixed in marble, representing both the people who resisted the Nazis, and those civilians who died during the bombing of Vienna. (16)

Niemalis Vergessen (Never Forget) Memorial

Location: Just north of the Hotel Sacher at Morzinplatz in Vienna, Austria.

Directions: From the Hotel Sacher walk north on Kartner Str. for 450 meters, then turn left on Singerstrasse, and then a quick right onto Rotenturmstasse for 450 meters. Turn left to Morzinplatz and you will see the monument.

Visit: This is an outdoor monument and is always open.

Mauthausen Concentration Camp

Location: About a 2-hour hour drive west of Vienna at Erinnerungsstraße 1, 4310 Mauthausen, Austria.

Directions: From the area of the Hotel Sacher drive to the A1 and follow it to St.Valentiner Str. Take exit 151-St.Valentin to the B1 toward Osterrcichische Romantikstrasse/B123. Follow signs to the memorial.

Visit: The camp is open from 9 am to 5:30 pm daily from March 1 to October 31. During the winter it closes at 3 pm. Check online for guided tours. They will charge for a minimum of 15 people. Entrance to the camp is free.

Website: https://www.mauthausen-memorial.org/en/

Additional Information: On August 9, 1938, prisoners from Dachau concentration camp near Munich were sent to the town of Mauthausen in Austria, to begin the construction of a new slave labor camp. (17) The site was chosen because of the nearby granite quarry, and its proximity to Linz. Although the camp was controlled by the German state from the beginning, it was founded by a private company as an economic enterprise.

Raoul Wallenberg Holocaust Memorial Park

Location: The memorial is located in the courtyard of the Dohany Street Synagogue in Budapest, at Budapest, Sip u. 10, 1075 Hungary.

Directions: It is about a 12-minute walk from the Kempinski Hotel. Turn left on Deak Ferenc, then turn right on Karoly krt. for about 300 meters, and then a left onto Dohany St. You will see the synagogue.

Visit: This is an outdoor memorial and can be visited anytime. It is best, however, to visit when the synagogue is open. The hours are in summer from 10 am to 7:30 pm and the rest of the year from 10 am to 5:30 pm.

Website: https://www.raoulwallenberg.net/wallenberg/tributes/world/hungary/

Additional Information: At least four hundred thousand Hungarian Jews were murdered by the Nazis.

Shoes on the Danube Bank Memorial

Location: Just north of the Marriott Hotel in Budapest, Hungary.

Directions: Walk north on Apaczai Csere Janos St. and continue along the river until you see the shoes on your left.

Visit: This is an outdoor memorial and can be visited anytime.

Website: https://en.wikipedia.org/wiki/Shoes_on_the_Danube_Bank

Additional Information: As many as twenty thousand Jews were murdered and thrown into the Danube river. (18)

The Carl Lutz Memorial

Location: Just north of the Dohany Street Synagogue in Budapest, Hungary.

Directions: Walk west from the Dohany Street Synagogue and then turn right onto Dob St.. The memorial will be on your left, in a small park adjacent to a building.

Visit: This is an outdoor memorial and is open everyday.

Website: https://hu.usembassy.gov/embassy/budapest/embassy-history/carl-lutz-memorial/

Additional Information: The inscription on the memorial reads: "In the building at Szabadság tér 12, Swiss Vice Consul Carl Lutz honorably represented the interests of the United States of America and other countries between 1942 and 1945. He courageously saved the lives of tens of thousands of Hungarian citizens persecuted as Jews."(19) The memorial was dedicated by the Embassy of the United States.

Memorial for the Victims of the German Occupation

Location: North of the Kempinski Hotel in Budapest, Hungary.

Directions: Walk north on October 6. u. for about 10 minutes and you will come to Liberty Square where the monument is located.

Visit: This is an outdoor monument and can be visited anytime.

Additional Information: "The Federation of Jewish Communities in Hungary (Mazsihisz) and other organizations have objected to the erection of the memorial, asserting that its depiction of Hungary as a quiescent and passive victim is inaccurate and serves to absolve the onetime Nazi ally from responsibility for its actions." (20)

Holocaust Memorial Center

Location: The memorials are located at the museum at 39 Pava St. in Budapest, Hungary.

Directions: From the Marriott Hotel walk south to Petofi ter and take the number 15 bus toward Boraros ter H for 4 stops to Koztelek utca and then walk south for 8 minutes on Ullot ut to Pava u. 39.

Visit: The museum is open from Tuesday to Sunday from 10 am to 6 pm. Telephone (+36)1 0 455-3333. Email at info@hdke.hu

Website: http://hdke.hu/en/

Additional Information: "The visitors are welcomed into a unique space that was named as the most impressive in Budapest by Frank Owen Gehry, one of the leading architects in our time. The modern building is organically linked to the Páva Street Synagogue, an authentic venue that once used to be the second largest site for Jewish worship in Budapest." (21)

Rumbula Forest Memorial

Location: About 8 miles south of the city center of Riga at Maskavas iela 471, Latgales priekšpilsēta, Rīga, LV-1063, Latvia.

Directions: The easiest way is to take an Uber to the memorial. You can also take the No. 18 bus to the Rumbula stop.

Visit: This is an outdoor memorial and may be visited anytime.

Website: http://memorialplaces.lu.lv/memorial-places/riga-and-riga-district/riga-rumbula/

Additional Information: The monument was paid for by a former ghetto prisoner by the name of Boris Kliot, whose parents were killed here. A path from the entrance leads to the central part of the memorial, which is shaped in the form of a star of David with a menorah above it. (22)

The Rumbula massacre is a collective term for incidents on November 30 and December 8, 1941, in which about twenty-five thousand Jews were killed, in or on the way to Rumbula forest near Riga during the Holocaust. Except for the Babi Yar massacre in Ukraine, this was the biggest two-day Holocaust atrocity until the operation of the death camps. (23)

Salaspils Labor Camp Memorial

Location: Approximately 12 miles south of Riga's city center at Salaspils novads, Salaspils pilsēta, LV-2117, Latvia.

Directions: The easiest way to get here is by Uber or private car. It is just south of the Rumbula memorial so both can be visited at the same time.

Visit: This is an outdoor memorial and can be visited anytime.

Website: https://www.atlasobscura.com/places/salaspils-memorial-ensemble

Additional Information: The camp was established at the end of 1941. Officially it was known as the Salaspils Police Prison and Re-Education Through Labor Camp. (24)

The Kielce Pogrom Denkmal (Memorial Plaque)

Location: In the central portion of Kielce, Poland at Planty 7, 25-508.

Directions: It is a few blocks from the Best Western Grand Hotel.

Visit: This is an outdoor memorial and can be visited anytime.

Website: https://en.wikipedia.org/wiki/Kielce_pogrom

The Umschlagplatz Monument

Location: Just northwest of Warsaw's Old Town at Stawki 10,00-178 Warsaw, Poland.

Directions: It is a 30 minute walk from the center of Warsaw's Old Town. Walk north on Miodowa for about 5 blocks and then turn left on Muranowska, continuing on Stawki and the destination will be on your left.

Visit: This is an outdoor memorial and can be visited anytime.

Website: https://sztetl.org.pl/en/towns/w/18-warsaw/116-sites-of-martyrdom/52343-umschlagplatz-miejsce-koncentracji-zydow-przed-wywozka-ul-stawki-10

Additional Information: During a two-month period between July 22 and September 21, 1941, approximately five to six thousand Jews were sent everyday from this spot to the Treblinka extermination camp, where they were murdered upon arrival. Any resistance in boarding the cattle cars was met with immediate death by shooting. (24)

Monument to the Ghetto Heroes

Location: Just northwest of Warsaw's Old Town at Ludwika Zamenhofa, 00-153 Warsaw, Poland.

Directions: It is a 20-minute walk from Warsaw's Old Town. Head north on Miodowa and turn left on Swietojerska until Ludwika Zamenhofa, then turn right. You will see the large monument on your left.

Visit: This is an outdoor memorial and can be visited anytime.

Website: https://sztetl.org.pl/en/towns/w/18-warsaw/116-sites-of-martyrdom/52389-warsaw-ghetto

Additional Information: During the summer of 1942 more than two hundred and fifty thousand Jews were deported from the ghetto to Treblinka and murdered. The remaining Jews formed a resistance group, built bunkers, and were able to smuggle in weapons from the outside. The uprising began on April 19, 1943, the evening before Passover. At that time the SS attempted to enter the ghetto for its complete liquidation. What was planned as a very short operation lasted almost a month and ended on May 16, 1943. A total of thirteen thousand died, mostly by suffocation or being burnt alive, during the block by block destruction of the ghetto. There were only one hundred and ten German casualties with sixteen killed. (25)

Mila 18 Memorial

Location: Just a block north of the Ghetto Heroes Memorial at Mila 2, 00-001 in Warsaw, Poland.

Directions: It is about a 23-minute walk from Warsaw's Old Town. Turn right (north) on Miodowa and walk for about 700 meters to Swietojerska and turn left. After 350 meters turn right on the second street. Make a left on Dubois and continue onto Mla. The monument will be on your right.

Visit: This is an outdoor memorial and can be visited anytime.

Website: https://sztetl.org.pl/en/ towns/w/18-warsaw/116-sites-of-martyrdom/52425-anielewiczs-bunker-mila-street

Additional information: In 1946, an obelisk was erected with inscriptions in Polish, Hebrew, and Yiddish on a mound of rubble of the previous headquarters of the resistance fighters. It states the following:

"On May 8, 1943, in this place Mordechaj Anielewicz—the commander of the Warsaw Ghetto Uprising died as a soldier, together with the staff of the Jewish Combat Organization and several dozen fighters of the Jewish resistance fighting against the German invaders." (26)

The Okopowa Street Jewish Cemetery

Location: The cemetery is located approximately 2 miles west of Warsaw's Old Town at Okjopowa 49/51,01-0-43 Warsaw, Poland.

Directions: It is easiest to take an Uber. It should be about a 10-minute ride.

Visit: The cemetery is open from 10 am to 5 pm Sunday to Thursday and 10 am to 3 pm on Friday. It is closed on Saturday.

Website: https://warszawa.jewish.org.pl/en/for-visitors/warsaw/okopowa/

Additional information: The cemetery was established in 1806 and is the resting place of over two hundred thousand Jews. It was placed on the register of historic buildings in 1973. (27)

Auschwitz Concentration Camp

Location: The camp is located approximately 40 miles west of the city of Krakow, Poland.

Directions: The best way to get there is by automobile or a tour. Take the A 4 west from Krakow and exit at Balin. Go south on Oświęcimska, DW933 and Krakowska to the camp parking lot.

Visit: There is no entrance fee to the site, but a guided tour is highly recommended. Tours should be booked at least two months in advance as there is a very high demand for these tours. The summer hours are from 8 am to 7 pm, the spring and fall hours are 9 am to 5 or 6 pm depending on the month. During winter the hours are from 9 am to 2 or 3 pm depending on the month.

Website: http://auschwitz.org/en/

Additional Information: Auschwitz was initially opened as a detention camp for political prisoners in May, 1940. In 1941, Rudolf Hoss met with Heinrich Himmler in Berlin. He was told by Himmler that Hitler had issued an order for the SS to solve the "Jewish Question." Hoss was appointed the commander of Auschwitz, which would become a major extermination camp in Poland. Zyklon B gas was utilized in the gas chambers, and the bodies were burnt in crematoria.

In October 1941, Birkenau was built about 1.8 miles from Auschwitz. Four gas chambers were utilized there to murder over one million Jews, seventy thousand Poles, twenty-five thousand Roma and fifteen thousand POWs. The infamous Josef Mengele conducted many brutal medical experiments there, including the famous twin experiments. There were also forty satellite camps that served as slave labor camps.

With the Soviet army approaching in January 1945, sixty thousand prisoners were forced to march to other locations.

Majdanek Concentration Camp

Location: The camp is located in the southeastern suburbs of Lublin, Poland, along the road leading to Zamość and Chełm.

Directions: From the city center you can take 23 bus or 156 trolleybus at the Krakowska Gate bus stop (Królewska Street) and 158 trolleybus next to the Saski Garden (a bus stop in Lipowa Street). All the buses stop in front of the entrance to the museum.

Visit: During the winter the museum is open daily from 9 am to 4 pm except for Mondays. During the summer the hours are extended until 6 pm. Guided tours are available and last about 2.5 hours.

Website: www.majdanek.eu/en

Additional Information: At the end of July 1941, Heinrich Himmler decided to build a concentration camp in Lublin, Poland. The camp was built in a southeastern suburb on the main road to Lvov. (16)

Approximately three hundred thousand people, representing over fifty nationalities, were imprisoned here. Forty-one percent of the inmates were Jewish and thirty-five percent were Polish. (17)

Eighty percent of the prisoners were murdered by starvation, mass executions by shootings, and gassing. The largest execution was of eighteen thousand Jewish prisoners on November 3, 1943, by machine gunning. (18)

Plaszow Concentration Camp

Location: The site is located about 4 miles south of Krakow, Poland.

Directions: The best way to visit is by car. Drive to the southern side of the camp and park on the side of the road across from Castorama on ul. Henryka Kamieńskiego, within view of the Memorial of Torn-Out Hearts. The address is Kamieńskiego 97, 30-555 Kraków, Poland.

Visit: This is an outdoor memorial and may be visited anytime.

Website: https://www.inyourpocket.com/krakow/kl-plaszow-concentration-camp-in-krakow_73759f

Additional information: The largest number of people confined here at any one time was twenty thousand. In 1944, Oskar Schindler moved his factory to the Sudetenland from this area and prevented the deportation of more than one thousand Jews. (19)

Amon Göth, the notorious camp commander portrayed in the movie *Schindler's List*, made life here unbearable. A prisoner was lucky to survive more than four weeks at the camp. (20)

The most significant memorial here is the Memorial of Torn-Out Hearts, which was designed by Witold Cęckiewicz and unveiled in 1964. This memorial depicts five figures that represent the five countries of Płaszów's victims. The large Polish inscription across the back of the monument reads, "To the memory of the martyrs murdered by the Nazi perpetrators of genocide in the years 1943-45." (22)

Treblinka Extermination Camp

Location: The camp is located approximately 60 miles northeast of Warsaw, Poland.

Directions: By automobile take the S8 north for 55 miles and exit at DW694. Drive 18 miles to the camp.

Visit: The grounds are open daily from 9 am to 6:30 pm as is the museum. To arrange for an English guide email: guide@muzeumtreblinka.eu

Website: https://muzeumtreblinka.eu/en/for-visitors/

Additional information: Treblinka was the third killing center developed by the Nazis, which was linked to a plan to murder two million Jews living in Poland. Operation Reinhard, as it was called, also included the killing centers of Belzec and Sobibor. The site is in a heavily wooded area that is hidden from public view. It was near the village of Wolka Okraglik, along a railway line for transportation to the camp. Between July and September of 1942, two hundred and sixty-five thousand Jews were deported from the Warsaw Ghetto and killed here. The average train had fifty to sixty cars. Carbon monoxide gas was delivered to the gas chambers via a large diesel engine. The camp was dismantled at the end of 1943. (21)

The Jewish Gratitude Memorial

Location: The memorial is located in Amsterdam, Holland, at the rear of the Hermitage Amsterdam, on Weesperstraat near the corner of Nieuwe Kerkstraat.

Directions: From the Holocaust Memorial it is a 10-minute walk. Walk west for 10 minutes onwards toward the Amstel river and you will see the memorial.

Visit: This is an outdoor memorial and can be visited at any time.

The National Holocaust Memorial

Location: The memorial will be redone as part of a new holocaust museum expected to reopen in 2023. It is located in the Jewish Cultural Quarter at Plantage Middenlaan 24 1018 DE Amsterdam, Holland.

Directions: From the Rijksmuseum take the metro number 19 east, for 5 stops, to the Alexanderplein stop. Walk for about 9 minutes to Plantage Middenlaan 24.

Visit: The site is part of the Jewish Cultural Quarter ticket, which enables you to visit all the Jewish sites. It is open from 11 am to 5 pm daily.

Website: https://jck.nl/en/location/national-holocaust-memorial

Additional Information: Otherwise known as the Hollandsche Schouwburg (Dutch Theater), it was opened

in 1892 as a theater. In 1941, the Nazis renamed the theater to the Joodse Schouwburg or Jewish Theater. "From that point on only Jewish actors and artists were allowed to perform—for a strictly Jewish audience. Inadvertently, this however did lead to the theater becoming a breeding ground of high level Jewish culture, with many Jewish orchestras, cultural organizations, and theater companies being formed and performing." (23) In July of 1942, the Nazis began using the location as a deportation center.

The Shadow Canal Memorials

Location: The canal is located in the Jewish quarter near the Amstel river in Amsterdam, Holland. The address is Nieuwe Keizersgracht 13-1, 1018 DR Amsterdam.

Directions: From the National Holocaust Memorial head northwest on Plantage Middenlaan for about 100 m. Turn left on Plantage Parklaan. After about 180 m you will be at the canal. Turn right and continue until you see the plaques.

Visit: This is an outdoor memorial and can be visited at any time.

The Dockworker Statue

Location: The statue is located in a small park, just outside the Portuguese Synagogue in Amsterdam, Holland.

Directions: Find the Portuguese Synagogue and go to the park to the right of the synagogue, where you will find the statue.

Website: https://en.wikipedia.org/wiki/February_strike

Visit: This is an outdoor memorial and can be visited at any time.

Women of Ravensbruck Memorial

Location: The memorial is located at the east side of the Museumplein in Amsterdam, Holland.

Directions: Walk in an easterly direction from the entrance to the Van Gogh museum and you will see the monument.

Visit: This is an outdoor memorial and can be visited at any time.

The Jewish Resistance Monument

Location: The memorial is located near the Jewish quarter, on the edge of the Amstel river at Amstel, 1011 PT Amsterdam, Netherlands.

Directions: From the Portuguese Synagogue walk southeast on Nieuwe Amstelstraat for about 200 meters and then make a right on Amstel. Continue on Amstel for about 200 meters until you see the monument.

Visit: This is an outdoor memorial and can be visited at any time.

Westerbork Concentration Camp Memorial

Location: The camp memorial is located approximately 110 miles northeast of Amsterdam, Holland at Oosthalen 8, 9414TG Hooghalen.

Directions: From Amsterdam take the A1 southeast to the A29 north for 100 miles. Take exit 31 at Westerbork to NN381 east. Then take the first exit onto Eursing and then continue on Beilerweg. Turn right on Oosthalen and the destination will be seen in 1 mile on your right.

Visit: The site is well organized. You must take a bus from the visitor center, which includes a small museum, to the site. The site is open from 10 am to 5 pm daily. A ticket costs ten euros.

Website: https://encyclopedia.ushmm.org/content/en/article/westerbork

Additional information: "The Dutch government established a camp at Westerbork in October 1939 to intern Jewish refugees who had entered the Netherlands illegally. The camp continued to function after the German invasion of the Netherlands in May 1940. In 1941 it had a population of 1,100 Jewish refugees, mostly from Germany."(24) Anne Frank was a prisoner here before being transferred to Bergen Belsen.

Amersfoort Concentration Camp

Location: The camp is located 30 miles southeast of Amsterdam, Holland, at Loes van Overeemiaan 19,3832 RZ Leusden, Netherlands.

Directions: From Amsterdam take the A10 for 3 miles to the A1 south, and merge onto the A28. Take exit 5 and then turn left on Leusderweg, quickly turning right on Laan 1914. Turn left onto Loes van Overeemlaan and the camp will be on your left.

Visit: The camp is open 7 days a week and there are guided tours available. The hours are from 9 am to 5 pm, depending on the season and day, so please check before you go.

Website: https://www.kampamersfoort.nl/en/

Additional information: Between 1941 and 1945, approximately 37,000 prisoners, mainly political prisoners, were incarcerated for varying lengths of time in this camp, which served as both a transit and prison camp under the direct command of the SS.(25)

Rusthof or Russian Field of Honor

Location: The cemetery is located about a 3-minute drive from the Amersfoort concentration camp at Dodeweg 31, 3832 RE Leusden, Netherlands.

Directions: From Amersfoort camp head NE on Lots

van Overeemlaan and turn right on Laan 1914. Continue onto Dodeweg until you come to the cemetery.

Visit: This is an outdoor memorial and can be visited during daylight hours.

Memorial Synagogue on Pokionnaya Hiss

Location: In a large park approximately 7 miles west of the Kremlin in Moscow at Kutuzovsky Ave, 53, Moscow, Russia, 121096

Directions: It is best to take a guide. If you take the metro the stop in Park Popedy

Visit: It is open from 10am to 5pm daily except Saturday and Monday.

Website: https://en.wikipedia.org/wiki/Holocaust_Memorial_Synagogue_(Moscow)

The Grieving Man

Location: The monument is located in a park about 12 miles south of central St. Petersburg at Moskovskaya Ulitsa, 5, St Petersburg, Russia, 196601.

Directions: The best way to visit is with a guide and driver. If you don't have a driver, take the 6371 train from the Vitebsky railway station to Pushkin (7 stops), exiting at Stantsiya Tsarskoye Selo. Walk for one minute to the Pushkin bus stop and take the number 386 bus for 6 stops, exiting at Moskovskaya street. Walk northwest for 500 meters and you will see the monument.

Visit: This is an outdoor memorial and can be visited anytime.

Website: https://www.prlib.ru/en/node/356303

Additional information: Also called "The Formula of Sorrow."

Pinkas Memorial Synagogue

Location: The synagogue is located in the old Jewish quarter next to the famous Jewish cemetery in Prague, Czech Republic.

Directions: From the Charles Bridge (Karlov most), head east and turn left on Krizovnicka, for 300 meters. Then turn right onto Kaprova and left onto Valentinska and you will come to the Synagogue at Siroka 23, 110 00 Josefov, Czechia.

Visit: This is part of the Jewish Museum tour and only one ticket is required. The hours are daily from 9 am to 4:30 pm, except during spring and summer, when it is open until 6 pm.

Website: https://www.jewishmuseum.cz/en/info/visit/opening-hours/

Additional information: This is the second-oldest preserved synagogue in Prague. It was restored from 1950–1954. From 1955 until 1960 the synagogue was transformed into a memorial. After the Russian invasion in 1968, the memorial was closed to the public for more than 20 years. (26) The 80,000 "names inscribed on the walls are placed in groups according to the victim's last place of residence prior to their arrest or deportation and are listed in alphabetical order." (26) There is also a permanent exhibition on the first floor of the Children's Drawings from the Terezin Ghetto.

The Stara Synagogue Memorial

Location: The memorial is approximately 54 miles southwest of Prague at Smetanovy sady 80/5, 301 00 Plzeň 3, Czechia.

Directions: From Prague follow D5/E50 to Route 26 in Ejpovice (exit 67). Continue on Route 26. Drive to Smetanovy sady in Plzeň.

Visit: Tours of the old synagogue occur from Sunday to Friday from 10 am to 6 pm except for Jewish holidays.

Website: https://www.pilsen.eu/tourist/visit/the-best-from-pilsen/great-and-old-synagogue/the-great-and-old-synagogues.aspx

Additional information: The memorial exists within the remnants of the walls of the Old Jewish School, which was built in 1875.

The stones are lined alphabetically in a structure designed by Petr Novak, an artist and professor at the local art school. (29)

Theresienstadt Concentration Camp

Location: The camp is located 30 miles north of Prague, Czech Republic, at Principova alej 304, 411 55 Terezín, Czechia.

Directions: By car take the E55 north to exit 35, merging onto route 608 north until you arrive at the camp.

Visit: The camp opens at 8 am and closes at 4:30 pm in the winter and 6 pm in the summer. Guided tours are available and take about two hours.

Website: https://www.pamatnik-terezin.cz/

Additional information: Terezin was originally a vacation resort for Czech nobility. It is within the walls of the Theresienstadt fortress, created by Emperor Joseph II of Austria. (27) The Gestapo, in 1940, converted Terezin into a Jewish ghetto and concentration camp. More than one hundred and fifty thousand Jews were sent here. (27)

During June of 1944 the International Red Cross visited the camp and was duped by the Nazis into believing that the conditions were more than adequate for the prisoners. (28)

The camp was also known for a highly developed cultural life despite the horrendous living conditions. (28)

Memorial to the Martyrs of the Deportation

Location: In Paris, France, in a small park behind the Cathedral of Notre Dame.

Directions: From the entrance to the Cathedral walk northeast until the first intersection and then make a right turn on Rue du Cloitre-Notre-Dame. After approximately 200 yards turn right on Quai aux Fleurs and you will come to the memorial at Square de l'lle-de- France.

Visit: The memorial is open from 10 am to 5 pm during the winter and until 7 pm during the summer months.

Website: https://en.wikipedia.org/wiki/Mémorial_des_Martyrs_de_la_Déportation

Additional information: Shaped like a ship's prow and thought of as a crypt, the memorial is entered through one of two staircases. There are two chapels containing earth and bones from concentration camps. (30) Inside the "crypt" is the tomb of an unknown deportee who was murdered in a concentration camp. Along both walls of the inner chamber are two hundred thousand glass crystals, meant to symbolize the deportees who were murdered in the camps. It was listed as one of the "14 Famous Monuments and Memorial Buildings Around the World" in *Architectural Digest* in 2018. (31)

Memorial of the Shoah

Location: In Paris, France, a short walk from Notre Dame Cathedral in the Le Marais district.

Directions: From Notre Dame turn right onto Rue du Cloitre-Notre-Dame for 100 meters and then turn left onto Pont Saint-Louis. Cross the bridge and turn right on Quai de l'Hotel de ville. At the next intersection turn left on Rue Geoffroy l'ashier. You will see the Memorial and Museum on your left after one block at 17 rue Geoffroy l'ashier, 75004 Paris.

Visit: The memorial and museum are open daily except for Saturday from 10 am to 6 pm and until 10 pm on Thursday. There is no charge for admission.

Website: http://www.memorialdelashoah.org/en/the-memorial/presentation/the-history-of-the-shoah-memorial.html

Additional information: The memorial also houses the Holocaust museum, a crypt containing the ashes of victims from death camps and the Warsaw Ghetto, and Jewish files created by the Vichy government. (32)

The Shoah Memorial Monument in Drancy

Location: Approximately 8 miles north of Paris Centrum and is best reached by using public transportation.

Directions: From the Saint-Michel Notre Dame rail station, take the RER B toward the Gare de Mitry Claye for 5 stops. Exit Le Bourget and walk east on Rue Etienne Dolet to the bus stop and take the number 143 bus toward Rosny-Sous-Bois for 6 stops to the Square de la Liberation. You will see the monument across the street at 110-112 avenue Jean-Jaures, 93700 Drancy.

Visit: The outdoor memorial is always open, but the inside spaces are open daily from 10 am to 6 pm except for Friday and Saturday.

Website: http://drancy.memorialdelashoah.org/en/

Additional information: During the 1930s, a low-income housing project was built in Drancy, called the Cite de la Muette. It was never completed. In 1941 it became an internment camp for Jews, prior to sending them to the extermination camps. "From December 1941 to March 1942, hostages were regularly removed from the camp and shot at Mont-Valerien or deported in retaliation for actions by the resistance." (33) There are permanent and temporary exhibitions in the building.

The Road to Death (Raoul Wallenberg Memorial)

Location: In Berzelii Park at the harbor in Stockholm, Sweden.

Directions: At the end of the Nybroviken (or New Bridge Bay) you will see Berzelii Park. The memorial faces the harbor.

Visit: This is an outdoor memorial and can be visited at any time.

Website: https://www.raoulwallenberg.net/wallenberg/tributes/world/sweden/

Additional information: The "road or way" is made up of cobblestones and was created as a direct link between the Holocaust Memorial and the Wallenberg Monument. (34)

The Stockholm Holocaust Memorial

Location: In the courtyard of the Great Synagogue in Stockholm, Sweden.

Directions: From Nybroviken head northwest on Strandvagen continuing on Nybroplan. Turn left at Birger Jarlsgaten, walk through Berzelii Park, and turn right on Nybrokajien, for about 20 yards. The synagogue will be on your right at 3, Wahrendorffsgatan, 111 47 Stockholm.

Visit: The courtyard is open weekdays. Contact the synagogue for more specific information.

Website: https://www.thelocal.se/20170803/the-stockholm-holocaust-memorial-a-restoration-of-human-dignity-and-a-warning-against-inhumanity

Additional information: The memorial was dedicated in 1998 by Carl Gustaf XVI, King of Sweden, and contains more than 8,000 names of victims who were relatives of Swedish Jews. (35)

The Never Again for Any Nation Memorial (For the Jews)

Location: In a small square in the city of Corfu, Greece, approximately a 20-minute walk from the cruise ship harbor.

Directions: From the cruise ship harbor turn left on Antistaseos and continue for about 350 yards and again turn left on El. Venizelou. After 700 yards turn right onto Str. Xenofontos. The memorial will be on your right at Str. Xenofontos 2, Kerkira 491 00.

Visit: This is an outdoor memorial and may be visited at any time.

The Monument to the Victims of the Holocaust

Location: In Ghetto Nuovo Square in the Jewish ghetto of Venice, Italy.

Directions: From St. Mark's square, it is about a 25-minute walk. You can put the address in your GPS as Campo di Ghetto Nuovo, 30100 Venezia, Italy.

Visit: As this is an outdoor monument, it can be visited at any time.

Website: https://bestveniceguides.it/en/2019/01/18/signs-of-remembrance-the-shoah-in-venice/

Additional Information: The monument was created in 1980 and consists of seven bronze panels. Approximately 1,200 out of the 1,443 Jews living in Venice escaped thanks to Giuseppe Jona, who burned a list of Jews before taking his own life. (36)

Deportation Monument

Location: Just outside the walls of the Akershus Fortress in Oslo, Norway.

Directions: The chair monument is located just outside the walls of the Fortress facing the harbor.

Visit: As this is an outdoor monument, it can be visited at any time.

Website: https://www.hlsenteret.no/gormley/english.html

Additional information: The chairs are outside the walls of the Fortress, representing the exclusion of Jews from Norwegian society during Nazi rule. (37)

The Hope Square Memorial

Location: In London, England just outside the Liverpool Station.

Directions: Take either the Central, Circle or Metropolitan line to the Liverpool station and exit at the south side.

Visit: This is an outdoor memorial and can be visited at any time.

Website: https://exploring-london.com/tag/hope-square/

Holocaust Memorial, Melbourne Holocaust Museum

Location: Forms the facade of the Melbourne Holocaust Museum in Melbourne, Australia.

Directions: From Queen Victoria Market it is about a 25-minute drive. Follow State Route 60 to Glen Huntly Rd in Elsternwick. Continue to Selwyn St. The address is 13-15 Selwyn St., Elsternwick Vic 3185.

Visit: As this is an outdoor monument, it can be visited at any time. For museum hours see the website.

Website: https://mhm.org.au/

The Memorial to the Holocaust of the Jewish People Montevideo

Location: On the shores of the River Plate, in Montevideo, Uruguay.

Directions: From the Old Town of Montevideo it is a 10-minute taxi ride along the shores of the River Plate eastward to 11200 Montevideo, Departamento de Montevideo.

Visit: As this is an outdoor monument, it can be visited at any time.

Website: https://en.turismojudaico.com/contenido/7/Holocaust-memorial-in-the-montevideo-river-boulevard

Additional information: "Upon approaching the monument one can see rail tracks that reference the road without return towards extermination camps. These tracks suggest the beginning of a descending path through a ramp that reaches a wall that may evoke the Western Wall, a strong symbol of Jewish world." (38)

Santa Clara Holocaust Memorial

Location: Approximately 170 miles east of Havana in the Jewish cemetery of Santa Clara, Cuba.

Directions: It is a 3-hour car ride on the A1 east from Havana. It would be best to take a guide.

Visit: As this is an outdoor monument, it can be visited at any time. It may be closed on the Sabbath.

Website: https://www.jta.org/2004/05/03/lifestyle/polish-stone-for-cubas-shoah-memorial

Havana Holocaust Memorial

Location: Approximately 10 miles east of the Hotel Melia Cohiba in Havana, Cuba.

Directions: It is best to take a guide and a car.

Visit: Daily except for the Sabbath.

Website: https://www.jewishvirtuallibrary.org/cuba-virtual-jewish-history-tour

Yad Vashem

Location: On the western slopes of Mt.Herzl in Jerusalem, Israel.

Directions: From the area of the King David Hotel it is a 15-minute taxi ride.

Visit: Monday through Thursday from 9 am to 4 pm; on Fridays it closes at 3 pm.

Website: https://www.yadvashem.org/

Canadian Society for Yad Vashem Holocaust Memorial Site

Location: In Earl Bales Park about 9 miles north of the city center of Toronto, Canada.

Directions: From the city center drive north on Bathurst St. for 9 miles and then turn right into Raoul Wallenberg Rd. The park is located at hurst St., North York, Ontario.

Visit: As this is an outdoor monument it can be visited at any time.

Website: https://yadvashem.ca/csyv-holocaust-memorial

The Holocaust Memorial Park in Brooklyn, N.Y.

Location: In Sheepshead Bay, Brooklyn, New York.

Directions: From the Port of Authority in Manhattan, take the A train toward Ozone Park for 3 stops, to W

4 St. Washington Square. Change to the B train toward Brighton Beach for 10 stops, exiting at Sheepshead Bay. Walk south on Sheepshead Bay Rd for about a half mile until you reach the bay. Turn right on Emmons Ave. and continue until you come to the park on West End Ave.

Visit: As this is an outdoor monument, it can be visited at any time.

Website: https://www.nycgovparks.org/parks/holocaust-memorial-park-bt10

Additional information: The park was dedicated in 1985 by the then-mayor, Edward Koch. The memorial was designed by George Vellonakis.

The New England Holocaust Memorial

Location: Near Faneuil Hall in Boston, Massachusetts.

Directions: It is a 3-minute walk from Faneuil Hall. Head west on Clinton St., then turn left onto North St., and then right onto Union St. Walk to 98 Union St.

Visit: As this is an outdoor monument, it can be visited at any time.

Website: https://www.nehm.org

Liberation Memorial in Liberty Park

Location: In Liberty Park, New Jersey, just south of Jersey City.

Directions: From Manhattan take the Holland tunnel (I 78) to New Jersey. Follow I 78 W toward I 95/Turnpike. Take exit 14 B toward Jersey City/Liberty State Park. The address is 200 Morris Pesin Dr., Jersey City.

Visit: As this is an outdoor monument, it can be visited at any time.

Website: https://en.wikipedia.org/wiki/Liberation_(Holocaust_memorial)

Baltimore Holocaust Memorial

Location: Four blocks from Baltimore, Maryland's Inner Harbor.

Directions: Walk east along E Pratt St. and then turn left on S Gray St. for two blocks. Turn right on E Lombard St. and left on S Frederick St. The memorial will be on your left.

Visit: As this is an outdoor monument, it can be visited at any time.

Website: http://www.josephsheppard.com/Holocaust/NewMemorial.htm

Additional information: A large concrete triangle forms the center plaza of the memorial. The sculpture stands at the apex of the triangle. A plaque, inscribed by Dr. Deborah Lipstadt, stands behind the sculpture and describes the events of the Holocaust. (39)

South Carolina Holocaust Memorial

Location: Near downtown Columbia, South Carolina.

Directions: Drive to the Memorial Park at 700 Hampton St., Columbia, SC 29201.

Visit: As this is an outdoor monument, it can be visited at any time.

Website: https://www.historiccolumbia.org/online-tours/vista/700-hampton-street

Additional information: The monument was dedicated in 2001.

Miami Holocaust Memorial

Location: One block west of the Miami Beach Convention Center in Miami Beach, Florida.

Directions: From Lincoln Road walk north on Washington Ave. for two blocks and then turn left on 17th

St.. Turn right on Convention Center Dr. and walk two blocks to 19th St. and turn left. The memorial will be on your right at 1933-1945 Meridian Avenue. It is a 10-minute walk.

Visit: The memorial is open from 9:30 am to sunset daily.

Website: https://holocaustmemorialmiamibeach.org

Additional information: Coincidentally, the physical address 1933-1945 matched the years of the Nazi regime. Many people felt that the site was "bashert." (40) Kenneth Treister, an architect, designed the memorial, and it was dedicated on February 4, 1990. It took four years to build. The sculptures were cast in Taiwan and Mexico City.

Nashville Holocaust Memorial

Location: Approximately 10 miles southwest of downtown Nashville, Tennessee, on the campus of the Gordon Jewish Community Center.

Directions: Take 70S/Harding Pike to Percy Warner Blvd and continue to the memorial at 801 Percy Warner Blvd., Nashville, TN 37205.

Visit: As the memorial is on the campus of the Jewish Community Center, phone for the hours and admission policy, 615-354-1679.

Website: http://nashvilleholocaustmemorial.org

Additional information: The sculpture was designed by Alex Limor and dedicated in October 2006.

New Orleans Holocaust Memorial

Location: On the banks of the Mississippi River in New Orleans, Louisiana, in Woldenberg Park.

Directions: Head northeast on Bourbon St. for one block and then turn right onto Bienville St. Walk 0.4

miles and you will see the park and memorials on the banks of the river.

Visit: This is an outdoor monument that can be visited at any time.

Website: https://jewishnola.com/jewish-new-orleans/new-orleans-holocaust-memorial

Additional information: The memorial was dedicated in June 2003.

Dallas Holocaust Memorial

Location: Eleven miles north of downtown Dallas on the campus of the Aaron Family JCC.

Directions: Drive north on Interstate 75 for 9 miles and take exit 8 A/N Central expressway. Continue for 1 mile to the Aaron Family JCC at 7900 Northaven Rd.

Visit: As this is on the campus of the JCC call 214-739-2737 for the hours.

Website: https://jccdallas.org

Houston Holocaust Museum Memorial

Location: In the Museum District of Houston, Texas.

Directions: It is a 10-minute drive from downtown Houston. Drive south on Fannin St for 2.6 miles and turn left onto Southmore Blvd.. After two blocks turn right on Caroline St. and then left onto Calumet St. The museum will be on your left at 5401 Caroline St., Houston, TX.

Visit: The memorial is built into the facade of the Houston Holocaust Museum and can be seen anytime. There are other memorials inside the museum as well. Call 713-942-8000 for more information.

Website: https://hmh.org

Additional information: The museum first opened

in 1996 and was doubled in size in 2019. It is the fourth-largest Holocaust museum in the United States. (41) The Memorial Room or Wall of Tears is located in the far back corner and is a place for meditation.

The Jewish Federation of San Antonio

Location: In the Jewish Federation building in San Antonio, Texas.

Directions: Take I-10 West to I-410 East for 9 miles to exit 19 and take FM 1535 N to 12500 NW Military Hwy #200, San Antonio.

Visit: Call 210-302-6960 for further information.

Website: https://www.jfsatx.org

Holocaust Memorial Center Detroit

Location: In the Farmington Hills suburb of Detroit, Michigan.

Directions: From downtown Detroit take M-10 north to Farmington Hills. Take exit 5 from I-696 W and follow Orchard Lake Rd to the Holocaust Memorial Center at 28123 Orchard Lake Road.

Visit: The memorial is built into the facade of the Holocaust Memorial Center so it can be seen at any time. Call 248-553-2400 for more information.

Website: https://www.holocaustcenter.org

Additional information: The Center was the first free-standing institution of its kind in the United States. (42) It was opened and dedicated in October 1984. In 2003, a new museum, resembling a Nazi death camp, was built on a nine-acre site. (43).

Skokie Holocaust Monument

Location: In Skokie, which is a northern suburb, approximately a 30-minute drive north of Chicago, Illinois.

Directions: From downtown Chicago take I-90 to I-94 W. After approximately 16 miles take exit 39A to Touhy Ave. Make a right on Niles Center Rd and then a left on Oakton St. The memorial is in a park opposite the library at 5213 Oakton St., Skokie.

Visit: This is an outdoor monument, so it can be visited at any time.

Illinois Holocaust Museum Memorial

Location: In Skokie, Illinois, a suburb of Chicago, located at 9603 Woods Drive.

Directions: It is an approximately 45-minute drive from the Magnificent Mile in Chicago to the museum. Take I 90 north to I 94 north and exit at Old Orchard Road in Skokie. Turn left (west) for one block to Woods Drive and turn left again. Drive for two minutes to the museum.

Visit: The museum is open Wednesday through Sunday from 10 am to 5 pm. Free parking is available.

Website: https://www.ilholocaustmuseum.org/programs-events/?category=public-tours&tag=virtual

Iowa Holocaust Memorial

Location: On the grounds of the Iowa State Capitol in Des Moines, Iowa.

Visit: As this is an outdoor monument, it can be visited at any time.

Website: http://www.iowaholocaustmemorial.com

Additional information: The memorial was built in

2013 by the Confluence landscape architectural firm of Des Moines. It was a gift of the Blank Fund. (44)

Kansas Memorial to the Six Million

Location: On the campus of the Kansas City JCC in Overland Park, Kansas.

Directions: From downtown Kansas City take the I-35 south to US 69 S/Overland Pkwy and merge onto I-435 E. Take exit 77A-B and continue on Nail Ave south to the JCC at 5801 W 115th St., Overland Park.

Visit: Call the JCC at (913) 327-8000

Website: https://mchekc.org/monument/

Additional information: The front of the sculpture depicts the Warsaw Ghetto uprising. "There are skeleton-like figures reaching out for remembrance and reverence of the Torah." (45)

Tucson Holocaust Memorial

Location: Approximately 7.2 miles northwest of downtown Tucson, Arizona.

Directions: Take E. Broadway Blvd east for 2.6 miles and then turn left on N Country Club Rd. After 3 miles turn right onto E Fort Lowell Rd. and then left on N Dodge Blvd. Drive to 3800 E River Rd.

Visit: Call ahead to the JCC at (520) 299 3000 as it is on the JCC property.

Website: https://tucsonjcc.org/jewish-living/holocaust-memorial/

Los Angeles Holocaust Monument

Location: Approximately 4 miles southeast of Hollywood.

Directions: From the intersection of Hollywood and Vine St., head south on Vine St. for 1.3 miles and take the right fork on N Rossmore Ave. Turn right onto Beverley Blvd. and turn left onto Grove Dr.. The destination will be at 100 Grove Dr., Los Angeles.

Visit: The site is outdoor in Pan Pacific Park and can be visited anytime, but there is an attached museum that has specified hours. Call (323) 651-3704 for more information.

Website: https://www.holocaustmuseumla.org/

Additional information: In 2010, a Holocaust museum opened next to the monument. It was designed by architect Hagy Belzberg. (46)

Desert Holocaust Memorial

Location: One mile north of the center of Palm Desert in Civic Center Park.

Directions: Drive to the southern edge of Civic Center Park with the entrance on Fred Waring.

Visit: This is an outdoor memorial and can be visited at any time.

Website: https://www.palmsprings.com/attractions/desert-holocaust-memorial/

San Francisco Holocaust Memorial

Location: Approximately 7 miles west of Fisherman's Wharf at 100 34th Ave, San Francisco.

Directions: Take US 101/Presidio Pkwy west for 4 miles to Ralston Ave. Continue on Ralston Ave and Take Kobbe Ave to Lincoln Blvd and drive to Camino Del Mar. The memorial is in front of the California Palace of the Legion of Honor.

Visit: This is an outdoor memorial and can be visited at any time.

Website: https://www.artandarchitecture-sf.com/sf-holocaust-memorial.html

Additional information: "The essential figure of the man standing at the fence is probably derived from Margaret Bourke-White's famous Life magazine 1945 photograph of the liberation of Buchenwald." (47)

Mercer Island Holocaust Memorial

Location: Approximately 7 miles east of downtown Seattle at the JCC on Mercer Island.

Directions: Take I-90 East to Mercer Island. Take exit 8/Mercer Way and continue to your destination at 3801 E Mercer Way, Mercer Island.

Visit: This is an outdoor memorial and can be visited at any time.

Website: https://www.si.edu/object/siris_ari_357272

Additional information: Also called the "Thou Shalt Not Forget" memorial.

Horwitz-Wasserman Holocaust Memorial Plaza

Location: In downtown Philadelphia a few blocks from the Barnes Foundation Museum.

Directions: From the Barnes Foundation Museum walk southeast halfway around Logan Circle and then continue for about three blocks to Levy Square. It is located at 16th Street and Benjamin Franklin Parkway.

Visit: This is an outdoor monument and may be visited at any time.

Website: https://www.philaholocaustmemorial.org

Ohio Holocaust and Liberators Memorial

Location: In Columbus, Ohio, on the grounds of the state capitol. The capitol is located at 1 Capitol Square, Columbus, OH 43215.

Directions: Drive to the 1 Capitol Square and you will see the monument just to the right of the capitol.

Visit: This is an outdoor memorial and can be visited at any time.

Website: https://www.ohiostatehouse.org/about/capitol-square/statues-and-monuments/ohio-holocaust-and-liberators-memorial

HOLOCAUST MUSEUMS

ARIZONA

The Tucson Jewish Museum and
    Holocaust center
564 S, Stone Avenue,
Tucson

CALIFORNIA

The Los Angeles Museum of the Holocaust
100 The Grove Drive
Los Angeles

FLORIDA

The Florida Holocaust Museum
55 Fifth Street South,
St. Petersburg

GEORGIA

The Breman Museum
1440 Spring Street NW
Atlanta
https://www.thebreman.org

ILLINOIS

Illinois Holocaust Museum and
    Education Center
9603 Woods Dr.
Skokie
https://www.ilholocaustmuseum.org/

INDIANA

Candles Holocaust Museum and
    Education Center
1532 South Third Street
Terre Haute
https://candlesholocaustmuseum.org

MICHIGAN

The Zekelman Holocaust Center
28123 Orchard Lake Road
Farmington Hills
https://www.holocaustcenter.org/visit/

MISSOURI

The Kaplan Feldman Holocaust Museum
36 Millstone Campus Drive
St. Louis
https://stlholocaustmuseum.org

NEW MEXICO

The New Mexico Holocaust Museum
616 Central Ave SW
Albuquerque
https://nmholocaustmuseum.org

NEW YORK

The Museum of Jewish Heritage
36 Battery Place
Manhattan
https://mjhnyc.org

The Holocaust Memorial and Tolerance Center
   of Nassau County
100 Crescent Beach Road
Glen Cove, Long Island
https://www.hmtcli.org

PENNSYLVANIA

The Holocaust Awareness Museum
   and Education Center
8339 Old York Road
Elkins Park
https://hamec.org

The Holocaust Center of Pittsburgh
Chatham University
0 Woodland Road,
Pittsburgh
https://hcofpgh.org

TEXAS

The Dallas Holocaust and Human
   Rights Museum
300 N Houston
Dallas
https://www.dhhrm.org

The El Paso Holocaust Museum
715 N.Oregon
El Paso
https://elpasoholocaustmuseum.org

The Holocaust Museum Houston

5401 Caroline
Houston
https://hmh.org

The Holocaust Memorial Museum
   of San Antonio
12500 NW Military Hwy
San Antonio
https://www.hmmsa.org/museum-history

WASHINGTON

The Holocaust Center for Humanity
2045 2nd Avenue
Seattle
https://www.holocaustcenterseattle.org/

WASHINGTON, D.C.

The United States Holocaust Memorial Museum
100 Raoul Wallenberg Place, SW
https://www.ushmm.org

VIRGINIA

The Virginia Holocaust Museum
2000 E Cary Streey
Richmond
https://www.vaholocaust.org/

REFERENCES

1. https://encyclopedia.ushmm.org/content/en/article/dachau

2. https://www.jewishvirtuallibrary.org/history-and-overview-of-dachau

3. https://www.dw.com/en/the-liberation-of-dachau-75-years-ago/a-53270700

4. https://www.scrapbookpages.com/DachauScrapbook/KZDachau/DachauLife01C.html

5. https://www.bavaria.by/experiences/city-country-culture/museums-galleries/jewish-centre-munich-and-synagogue-ohel-jakob/

6. https://www.kz-gedenkstaette-dachau.de/en/

7. https://www.germany.travel/en/towns-cities-culture/jewish-traveler/big-cities/munich.html

8. https://www.en.uni-muenchen.de/about_lmu/introducing-lmu/history/contexts/09_white_rose/index.html

9. https://www.weisse-rose-stiftung.de/white-rose-memorial-exhibition/

10. Knoch, Habbo (ed) (2010). Bergen-Belsen: Wehrmacht POW Camp 1940–1945, Concentration Camp 1943–1945, Displaced Persons Camp 1945–1950. Catalogue of the permanent exhibition. Wallstein. ISBN 978-3-8353-0794-0.

11. https://en.wikipedia.org/wiki/Buchenwald_concentration_camp/

12. https://en.wikipedia.org/wiki/Bullenhuser_Damm

13. http://www.jg-berlin.org/en/judaism/cemeteries/grosse-hamburger-strasse.html

14. https://www.visitberlin.de/en/sinti-and-roma-memorial

15. https://www.sachsenhausen-sbg.de/en/visitor-service/

16. Anna Wisniewska & Czeslaw Rajca, Majdanek, The Concentration Camp of Lublin (Panstwowe Muzeum Na Majdanku 2002), 6.

17. Anna Wisniewska & Czeslaw Rajca, Majdanek, 23.

18. Anna Wisniewska & Czeslaw Rajca, Majdanek, 42.

19. https://encyclopedia.ushmm.org/content/en/article/plaszow

20. https://www.jewishgen.org/forgottencamps/camps/plaszeng.html

21. https://encyclopedia.ushmm.org/content/en/article/treblinka

22. https://www.inyourpocket.com/krakow/c-dolek_112728v

23. https://europeanmemories.net/memorial-heritage/hollandsche-schouwburg-national-holocaust-memorial

24. https://encyclopedia.ushmm.org/content/en/article/westerbork

25. https://www.kampamersfoort.nl/en/

26. https://www.jewishmuseum.cz/en/explore/sites/pinkas-synagogue/

27. http://www.terezin.org/the-history-of-terezin

28. https://encyclopedia.ushmm.org/content/en/article/theresienstadt

29. http://samgrubersjewishartmonuments.blogspot.

com/2018/07/plzens-holocaust-memorial-combines-best.html

30. https://en.wikipedia.org/wiki/Mémorial_des_Martyrs_de_la_Déportation

31. https://www.architecturaldigest.com/gallery/memorial-architecture-slideshow

32. https://en.wikipedia.org/wiki/Mémorial_de_la_Shoah

33. http://drancy.memorialdelashoah.org/en/the-drancy-memorial/presentation/the-history-of-the-cite-de-la-muette.html

34. https://www.raoulwallenberg.net/wallenberg/tributes/world/sweden/

35. https://jewish-heritage-europe.eu/sweden/heritage-heritage-sites/

36. https://www.venetoinside.com/hidden-treasures/post/monument-to-the-victims-of-the-holocaust-in-ghetto/

37. https://www.hlsenteret.no/gormley/english.html

38. https://en.turismojudaico.com/contenido/7/Holocaust-memorial-in-the-montevideo-river-boulevard

39. http://www.josephsheppard.com/Holocaust/NewMemorial.htm

40. https://holocaustmemorialmiamibeach.org

41. https://hmh.org

42. http://www.iowaholocaustmemorial.com

43. https://www.kcfountains.com/single-post/2016/11/17/memorial-to-the-six-million

44. https://en.wikipedia.org/wiki/Holocaust_Museum_LA

45. https://www.artandarchitecture-sf.com/sf-holocaust-memorial.html

About the Author

FRED KATZ is a retired Radiologist, Associate Professor of Radiology at the Philadelphia College of Osteopathic Medicine, and an accomplished photographer. He is dedicated to the advancement of Judaica studies and preserving the legacies of those who perished in the Holocaust.

Dr. Katz served as a physician during the Vietnam War, receiving a Bronze Star and Army Commendation medal for his service during the war. During his time in Vietnam, he volunteered at a clinic in An Khe and a hospital in Quin Nohn. Those unforgettable experiences steered him to a path of communal and professional service and paved the foundation for this book, which has taken him around the world as he photographed over 100 memorials from Auschwitz to Moscow to New York.

As a devoted photographer, to perfect his skills, he completed the Rocky Mountain School of Photography's intensive course that led him to master all phases of photography, including the processing and digital editing of his photographs. His photographs have been exhibited at the Breman Jewish Museum, the Atlanta Jewish Community Center, and various synagogues. Katz is also an accomplished speaker, having lectured for the Jewish Federations of North America, radiological societies, and medical schools.